The Abe Administration and the Rise of the Prime Ministerial Executive

With the advent of the second Abe administration, the question of 'who leads' in Japan has become much easier to answer – the prime minister and his executive office, backed by a substantial policy support apparatus. The rise of the 'prime ministerial executive' is one of the most important structural changes in Japan's political system in the post-war period.

This book explains how the prime ministerial executive operates under the Abe administration and how it is contributing to Abe's unprecedented policymaking power. The book analyses how reform of central government under Prime Ministers Nakasone, Hashimoto and Koizumi produced the necessary institutional innovations to allow the prime minister to assert more authoritative policy leadership, turning Japan's traditional, decentralised and bottom-up policy process on its head. Comparing the Westminster and presidential models of governance and applying them to Japan's contemporary politics, the book shows that, whilst elements of both can be found, neither captures the essence of the transformation involved in the rise of the prime ministerial executive.

Providing a thorough analysis of power relations in Japanese politics, this book will be useful to students and scholars of Japanese Politics, Comparative Politics and Asian Studies.

Aurelia George Mulgan is Professor in the School of Humanities and Social Sciences at University of New South Wales, Canberra, Australia. Her publications include *Ozawa Ichirō and Japanese Politics: Old Versus New* (Routledge, 2014).

Routledge Focus on Asia

The Abe Administration and the Rise of the Prime Ministerial Executive

Aurelia George Mulgan

Routledge
Taylor & Francis Group

LONDON AND NEW YORK

First published 2018 by Routledge

2 Park Square, Milton Park, Abingdon, Oxfordshire OX14 4RN
52 Vanderbilt Avenue, New York, NY 10017

Routledge is an imprint of the Taylor & Francis Group, an informa business

First issued in paperback 2018

British Library Cataloguing-in-Publication Data
A catalogue record for this book is available from the British Library

Library of Congress Cataloging-in-Publication Data
Names: Mulgan, Aurelia George, author.
Title: The Abe administration and the rise of the prime ministerial
    executive / Aurelia George Mulgan.
Description: Abingdon, Oxon ; New York, NY : Routledge, 2018. | Series:
    Routledge focus on Asia ; 1 | Includes bibliographical references and
    index.
Identifiers: LCCN 2017017995 | ISBN 9781138105874 (hardback) |
    ISBN 9781315101736 (ebook)
Subjects: LCSH: Executive power—Japan. | Abe, Shinzåo, 1954– |
    Japan—Politics and government—21st century.
Classification: LCC JQ1640 .M85 2018 | DDC 952.05/12—dc23
LC record available at https://lccn.loc.gov/2017017995

ISBN: 978-1-138-10587-4 (hbk)
ISBN: 978-0-367-17530-6 (pbk)

Typeset in Times New Roman
by Apex CoVantage, LLC

Contents

Acknowledgements

I would like to acknowledge the continuing support of the Australian Research Council (ARC) Discovery Projects scheme, which has assisted my research with successive grants over a number of years. Without this funding, the book could not have been written. I am also greatly indebted to my research assistant, Yong Suk Koh, whose skills and dedication have contributed so much to this work. My husband, Richard Mulgan, as ever, has provided wise counsel and an index, both indispensable contributions to the book. To Brian Woodall, whose work remains an inspiration, I express my gratitude for being such a good academic mate and offering such insightful guidance on the manuscript. My thanks also to the anonymous reviewer for reading and commenting on the manuscript.

1   Introduction

Abe Shinzō has embarked 'on a journey to become a "great prime minister" (*daisōri*)'.[1] With an ambitious policy agenda encompassing Japan's economic revival, normalisation of its military posture and constitutional reform, the prime minister has displayed unsurpassed executive power across a range of policy areas including reform of Japan's security policy, restructuring the farm sector and agricultural cooperatives (Japan Agriculture, or JA), agreeing to the Trans-Pacific Partnership (TPP) and delaying two increases in the consumption tax. While many critics would argue that the Abe administration's policies have not been successful in reviving a moribund Japanese economy, all would agree that at least the prime minister has been decisive in executing them. No longer does Japan suffer from a 'chronic leadership vacuum'[2] or a 'political leadership deficit'.[3] No longer does it deserve the label 'leaderless state'.[4] The Abe prime ministership unequivocally demonstrates the 'politics of decision' (*kimerareru seiji*).[5]

One of the most important factors contributing to the Abe administration's policy achievements is the mobilisation of an extensive infrastructure of prime minister-led policymaking. Former Liberal Democratic Party (LDP) heavyweight and now leader of the People's Life Party, Ozawa Ichirō, first advocated such a 'comprehensive, strategic decision-making apparatus'[6] in his *Blueprint for a New Japan* more than two decades ago. This proposal has now come to fruition in the emergence of a so-called 'prime ministerial executive' comprising the prime minister and his executive office (known as the 'Kantei'), together with its policy and administrative support apparatus.

The rise of the prime ministerial executive in Japan represents the culmination of a series of 'systemic or institutional reforms' (*seido kaikaku*).[7] The most consequential of these was administrative reform (*gyōsei kaikaku*) incorporating central government reform, which constructed a strong 'institutional resource base'[8] for the exercise of prime ministerial power. Three of Abe's predecessors – Prime Minister Nakasone Yasuhiro, Prime Minister Hashimoto Ryūtarō and Prime Minister Koizumi Junichirō – played a key role in advancing the process of administrative reform by improving and expanding prime ministerial and cabinet support structures in their quest to exert more decisive influence over policy outcomes. The measures adopted to 'establish a system of more effective political leadership' – one of the four pillars of the 'administrative reform of the central government of Japan'[9] – furnished the necessary ingredients for the rise of the prime ministerial executive. Other political reforms reinforced this process but would not have been sufficient without the critical input of central government reform, which provided the requisite institutional framework for prime minister-led policymaking. The structural changes to the policymaking process allowed successive prime ministers to develop new modes of policy leadership.

Prime Minister Abe has taken this process further than any of his predecessors by fully deploying, expanding and diversifying the apparatus of assistance and support for the exercise of prime ministerial authority, including both official and unofficial personnel arrangements within his executive office and by creating new entities to buttress his executive power. In this way, Abe has been able to mount a strong challenge to well-established political and administrative conventions operating within the central government.

The prime ministerial executive in the Abe administration

While the prime minister and his executive office are widely known as the Kantei, this also refers to the Kantei building, or 'Prime Minister's Official Residence', which houses the prime ministerial offices.[10] In terms of personnel, the Kantei includes the prime minister, the chief cabinet secretary (*naikaku kanbō chōkan*), three (one administrative and two parliamentary) deputy chief cabinet secretaries (*naikaku kanbō fukuchōkan*), the prime minister's executive secretaries (*sōri hishokan*) and special advisers (*sōri hosakan*). These are the main personnel who work in the Kantei building. Support personnel are also referred to as 'Kantei staff' and include special advisers to the cabinet (*naikaku kanbō sanyo*) and three assistant chief cabinet secretaries (*naikaku kanbō fukuchōkan ho*).

Two important organisations that form the broader structure of assistance and support for the Kantei are the Cabinet Secretariat and the Cabinet Office, which share the same office building close to the Kantei. There is some overlap amongst all three bodies in terms of personnel, organisational composition and physical location. Cabinet Secretariat personnel who work most closely with the prime minister are located in the Kantei building,[11] while the rest work in the Cabinet Office building, including the assistant chief cabinet secretaries. Special advisers to the cabinet have their offices in either the Kantei or the Cabinet Office depending on the special adviser. In addition to its own executives (chief cabinet secretary, deputy chief cabinet secretaries etc.), the Cabinet Secretariat has an array of organisational subunits such as offices (*shitsu*), secretariats (*jimukyoku*) and headquarters (*honbu*) and also includes the 'ministers in charge (of certain issues)' (*tantō daijin*).

The Cabinet Office is officially headed by the prime minister, who is one of its ministers along with the chief cabinet secretary and 'ministers of state for special missions' (*tokumei tantō daijin*), together with three senior vice-ministers (*naikakufu fukudaijin*) and three parliamentary secretaries (*naikakufu seimukan*) who are also part of the executive team assisting the prime minister.[12] In addition, the Cabinet Office is the umbrella organisation for the five 'councils on important policies' (*juyō seisaku ni kansuru kaigi*) such as the Council on Economic and Fiscal Policy (CEFP) chaired by either the prime minister or the chief cabinet secretary,[13] as well as for numerous other councils, headquarters and committees etc. and contains a large complement of executive and support staff attached to its various bureaux, divisions etc. The Cabinet Secretariat and the Cabinet Office formally comprise the so-called 'core government offices centered on the prime minister'[14] and are, therefore, integral to the formal power resources available to the prime minister to buttress his executive leadership.

The cabinet as a collective entity and other bodies such as the ruling party executive are not part of the prime ministerial executive in terms of their formal roles and functioning. This is despite the fact that the Cabinet Secretariat formally works for both the prime minister and the cabinet, and the Cabinet Office is similarly tasked with 'assisting the prime minister *and his cabinet*' (emphasis added).[15] Some ministers individually, however, are part of the prime ministerial executive in their roles as Cabinet Office 'ministers of state for special missions' (who must also be state ministers, or *kokumu daijin*) and Cabinet Secretariat 'ministers in charge (of certain issues)'.

It is important in this context to distinguish between the 'formal political executive' and the 'prime ministerial executive'. The 'formal political executive' consists of the prime minister and the cabinet while the prime ministerial executive is made up of the prime minister and the Kantei as well as the 'core government offices'. In essence, it comprises the prime minister plus the 'organizational infrastructure around the prime minister',[16] in short, those institutions supporting his executive leadership on policy issues. The prime ministerial executive is not the equivalent of the 'core executive' despite its being depicted as such in the literature on Japanese politics.[17] The 'core executive', as formally defined,[18] also includes the cabinet as 'the supreme body in the core executive'[19] and key cabinet committees, not just the prime minister and the institutions and personnel supporting him.

Outline of the book

The book begins by providing a brief overview of the traditional model of Japanese policymaking and the role of the prime minister. It then traces the expanding power and functions of the prime ministerial executive consequent upon the series of central government reforms undertaken as part of the government-sponsored process of administrative reform, outlining the important contributions of the Nakasone, Hashimoto and Koizumi administrations. It also analyses the impact of other relevant political factors and developments, particularly electoral reform, and outlines where Abe went wrong during his first administration in 2006–2007 by not deploying the leadership power resources generated by administrative reform in a functional and efficient manner.

Abe's second administration (2012–) provides a glittering contrast to his first with the full flowering of the prime ministerial executive. The book highlights the concrete steps that Abe has taken to expand his executive authority, including adaptations and advancements in the institutional structures and arrangements provided by administrative reform and the deployment of new instruments of executive power. It also identifies other factors contributing to Abe's strong political leadership as prime minister, including his reliance on an 'inner core elite',[20] his judicious personnel appointments, his personal leadership capacity and other personal resource factors.

As part of the analysis, the book examines the changing nature of relations between the prime ministerial executive and other key elements of the Japanese government: the cabinet, cabinet ministers, the bureaucracy and the ruling party under both the Koizumi and Abe administrations, particularly in relation to potential constraints on the exercise of prime ministerial authority.

The book concludes by evaluating the broader, system-wide significance of the rise of prime ministerial executive in two main respects: the Westminsterisation of Japan's parliamentary cabinet system and the presidentialisation of the prime ministership. The book poses two fundamental questions about these potentially contrasting developments. First, because the policymaking system is now more centralised than decentralised and more top-down than bottom-up, can we say that Japan is becoming a more Westminster-style parliamentary cabinet system? Second, given the apparent ascendance of prime ministerial leadership, could it be argued that Japan's political system is instead moving in a more 'presidential' direction?

Notes

1 Mikuriya, Takashi, *Abe seiken wa hontō ni tsuyoi no ka* [*Is the Abe Administration Actually Strong?*], Tokyo, PHP Kenkyūjo, 2015, p. 217.

2 Fackler, Martin, 'In Japan, a Leadership Vacuum', *New York Times*, 2 September, 2008, www.nytimes.com/2008/09/03/world/asia/03japan.html.

3 George Mulgan, Aurelia, 'Japan's Political Leadership Deficit', *Australian Journal of Political Science*, Vol. 3, No. 2, 2000, pp. 183–202. Analysts have also referred to Japan's 'vacuum of political leadership'. Gannon, James and Sahashi, Ryo, 'Looking for Leadership', in Ryo Sahashi and James Gannon (eds), *Looking for Leadership: The Dilemma of Political Leadership in Japan*, Tokyo and New York, Japan Center for International Exchange, 2015, p. 12. See also Hosoya, Yuichi, 'The Evolution of Japan's "Leadership Deficit"', in Sahashi and Gannon (eds), *Looking for Leadership*, pp. 31–45.

4 Tokuyama, Jirō, 'Japan's Leaderless State', *Japan Echo*, Vol. 18, No. 4, 1991, pp. 35–41.

5 Mikuriya, *Abe seiken*, p. 207.

6 Ozawa, Ichirō, *Blueprint for a New Japan: The Rethinking of a Nation*, Tokyo, Kōdansha International, 1994, p. 25.

7 Uchiyama, Yū, 'Nihon seiji no akutā to seisaku kettei patān' ['Actors and Policymaking Patterns in Japanese Politics'], *Kikan Seisaku Keiei Kenkyū*, Vol. 3, Mitsubishi UFJ Research and Consulting, 2010, www.murc.jp/english/think_tank/quarterly_journal/qj1003_01.pdf, p. 11.

8 The term 'institutional resource base' is taken from Heffernan, Richard, *Presidentialization in the United Kingdom: Prime Ministerial Power and Parliamentary Democracy*, Paper prepared for delivery at the 28th Joint Sessions of Workshops of the European Consortium of Political Research, University of Copenhagen, 14 to 19 April 2000, https://ecpr.eu/Filestore/PaperProposal/9c85aa57-e9c7-45b9-bd92-2eb41282e737.pdf, p. 18. This analysis refers to the machinery of prime ministerial governance under Prime Minister Blair, which has strong parallels to the prime ministerial executive under Prime Minister Abe, viz., the strengthening of 10 Downing Street with separate divisions, including the Press Office, and the separate Cabinet Office 'revamped into an institution under the direction of Downing Street', which together combine into a 'Whitehall Centre'... "an executive office in all but name", [which] is increasingly the servant of a powerful Prime Minister' (p. 18).

9 The four pillars were listed in a December 2000 explanatory publication issued by the Headquarters for the Administrative Reform of the Central Government of Japan. Besides 'Establishing a System with more Effective Political Leadership', the others were: 'Restructuring National Administrative Organs', 'Creating a More Transparent Administration' and 'Drastically Streamlining the Central Government'. See National Science Foundation, Tokyo Regional Office, Report Memorandum #01–02, *Central Government Reform in Japan: Rationale and Prospects*, 9 February 2001, www.nsf.gov/od/oise/tokyo/reports/trm/rm01-02.html. The Report Memorandum also revealed that Koike Tadao, former president of the *Mainichi Shinbun*, former chairman of the Japan Newspaper Publishers and Editors Association and a member of the Advisory Council to the Headquarters for Administrative Reform, wrote that the first of these pillars was the most important and indeed, the effectiveness of the remaining three would depend critically on how seriously this first pillar was taken.

10 Despite the term 'Prime Minister's Official Residence', the prime minister's living quarters are in the Kōtei (the official residence of the prime minister) built next door to the Kantei.

11 Furukawa, Teijirō, 'Sōri kantei to kanbō no kenkyū – Taiken ni motozuite' ['A Study of the Prime Minister's Official Residence and Secretariat – Based on

Experience'], *Nenpo Gyōsei Kenkyū*, Vol. 2005, No. 40, 2005, www.jstage.jst. go.jp/article/jspa1962/2005/40/2005_2/_pdf, p. 3.

12 The official website of the Cabinet Office provides details of its organisational structure and personnel including the ministers of state, senior vice-ministers and parliamentary secretaries etc. See, *Cabinet Office, Outline of Duties, 2014*, June 2014, www.cao.go.jp/en/pmf/about_pmf_index.pdf.

13 The others are the Council for Science and Technology Policy, the Council on National Strategic Special Zones, the Central Disaster Management Council and the Council for Gender Equality. See *Cabinet Office*, www.cao.go.jp/en/pmf/about_pmf_index.pdf. See also below.

14 Takayasu, Kensuke, 'The Pressures of Change: The Office of Prime Minister in the United Kingdom and Japan', *Nippon.com*, 21 May 2014, www.nippon.com/en/features/c00410/.

15 'Overview: The Cabinet Office's Role in the Cabinet', *Cabinet Office, Outline of Duties 2014*, www.cao.go.jp/en/pmf/pmf_about.pdf.

16 Takayasu, 'The Pressures of Change', www.nippon.com/en/features/c00410/.

17 See, for example, Shinoda, Tomohito, 'Japan's Cabinet Secretariat and Its Emergence as Core Executive', *Asian Survey*, Vol. 45, No. 5, 2005, pp. 800–821.

18 As it was initially defined, 'core executive' refers to 'all those organizations and structures that primarily serve to pull together and integrate central government policies, or act as final arbiters within the executive of conflicts between different elements of the government machine.' Dunleavy, Patrick and Rhodes, R.A.W., 'Core Executive Studies in Britain', *Public Administration*, Vol. 68, 1990, p. 4. Although the components of the core executive varied depending on the policy issue, the key elements appeared to embrace the formal political executive. These elements were identified in later definitions, viz., 'The core executive refers to the complex web of institutions, networks and relations which embed the prime minister, cabinet, key cabinet committees and senior officials at the heart of the government machine.' McEwen, Nicola, 'Power within the Executive', Unit 2, Governing the UK, *BBC News*, 1 September 2003, http://news.bbc.co.uk/2/hi/programmes/bbc_parliament/2561931.stm. In fact, by some definitions, the 'core executive' also included the Senior Civil Service, which it does not in Japan, viz., 'The core executive is that part of government that implements policy. This covers the Prime Minister, the Cabinet, the Cabinet Committees, the Cabinet Office, the government departments and the Senior Civil Service.' 'Core Executive (UK Politics)', *tutor 2u*, www.tutor2u.net/politics/reference/core-executive-uk-politics.

19 Takayasu, Kensuke, 'Prime-ministerial Power in Japan: A Re-Examination', *Japan Forum*, Vol. 17, No. 2, 2005, p. 169.

20 Heffernan, *Presidentialization in the United Kingdom*, p. 24.

2 The rise of the prime ministerial executive and the process of administrative reform

Many analysts have commented on the weakness[1] and passivity[2] of Japanese prime ministers who have traditionally relied on decisions made from the bottom up.[3] Prime ministers have presided rather than decided[4] and have been widely regarded as 'incapable of demonstrating actual leadership in most areas.'[5] In *Blueprint*, Ozawa described the Japanese prime minister as 'nothing more than a master of ceremonies for the ritual at hand.'[6] He wrote, 'the hands and feet of the political structure were created, but the "brain" to govern them was not.'[7] If the prime minister did exercise policy leadership it was 'reactive'[8] rather than proactive. He[9] was a ratifier and arbiter,[10] facilitator and coordinator,[11] a 'judicious consensus-builder . . . rather than a forceful advocate of independently derived initiatives'.[12] As Uchiyama wrote, 'Japan's prime ministers generally worked more to coordinate and conciliate conflicting positions between the various ministries and within the party than to take the initiative in making policy decisions'.[13]

In this 'leaderless state', power was shared amongst bureaucratic and ruling party groups, but there was no pinnacle of power.[14] In other words, the system lacked 'a central authority for making coherent decisions.'[15] The cabinet, 'nominally Japan's supreme decision-making body . . . [was] an empty institution.'[16] Bureaucrats in the main ministries and LDP Diet politicians with specialist expertise and influence in specific policy areas – so-called 'tribe Diet members' (*zoku giin*) – were the principal players who made the key decisions. Policy was formulated in the ministries but was then subject to examination and approval by the ruling party in a dual system known as 'government-party' (*seifu-yotō*) policymaking.[17] Over time, routinised and institutionalised patterns of consultation, negotiation and mutual dependence developed amongst the *zoku giin*, bureaucrats and allied interest groups,[18] which led to the formation of so-called 'subgovernments', 'policy triangles' or 'iron triangles' in particular policy domains.[19]

In summary, Japan's traditional policymaking process was largely a decentralised, bottom-up, segmented system organised around specific areas of policy and reinforced by policy specialisation amongst LDP *zoku* and bureaucratic sectionalism in the main ministries. It was an 'un-Westminister' system[20] with a 'weak cabinet'[21] and a weak prime minister, with ruling party Diet members exercising influence 'outside the cabinet',[22] and with close working relations amongst the *zoku*, bureaucrats and interest group leaders in segregated policy domains. In practice, the formal political executive comprising the prime minister and cabinet faced the *de facto* veto power of the LDP and the bureaucracy,[23] which prevented it from leading the government.

Over the years, however, Japanese prime ministers have exercised evergreater power over government policy. Importantly, this trend has embraced not just the expanding power of the prime minister himself but also the prime minister *and his office* – the supporting structures of executive governance centring on the Kantei[24] – for so long, 'little more than an onlooker in the actual policymaking process'.[25] Not only has the prime ministerial executive acquired greater authority in determining policy outcomes, but this has also been matched by the relative decline in the policymaking influence of bureaucrats, *zoku* legislators and their associated 'policy triangles'. Over time, 'bottom-up' has gradually given way to 'top-down' and 'vertically segmented' has given way to 'horizontally centralised'.

The process began as an attempt by a number of prime ministers to bolster their own power. They set about consciously changing the policymaking process by promoting central government reform, including the establishment of new institutions, procedures and conventions of policymaking. Three prime ministers were pivotal in this regard: Prime Minister Nakasone Yasuhiro (1982–1987), Prime Minister Hashimoto Ryūtarō (1996–1998) and Prime Minister Koizumi Junichirō (2001–2006).[26]

Each shared an ambition to exert decisive influence over policy outcomes. For Nakasone and Koizumi, this ambition was accompanied by a strong determination to reduce the power of the countervailing blocs in the policymaking system. In Nakasone's case, it was primarily 'the bureaucrat-centered political system',[27] while for Koizumi, it was a desire to vanquish anti-reform elements within his own party and in the bureaucracy. In Hashimoto's case, it was sheer frustration with the limits of his power and the thought that 'The prime minister must be strong.'[28] As Mikuriya relates,

> [T]he first thing Hashimoto was told by people around him the instant he was appointed as prime minister was 'what a prime minister must not do'. He was given a long list of things over which he 'did not have exclusive right'. It is said that an enraged Hashimoto said, 'Why is the first thing I hear when I become prime minister a list of things I can't do? What you should be telling me are the things that you want me to do and things that I can definitely do!' This is not surprising at all. The

prime minister and party leader – the one person with supreme power – was bound hand and foot and could not actually do anything. Hashimoto wanted to change that.[29]

Both Nakasone and Koizumi also shared the view that the prime minister should be popularly elected rather than chosen by the parliament in an attempt to formalise their power base in the national electorate. Both, however, had to settle for using the institutional power resources that were available to them as the main foundation of their authority, combined with direct popular appeals. In Nakasone's case, the former were more limited, while Koizumi's long-term administration was based on a much stronger institutional foundation.[30] Together with Hashimoto, all three prime ministers had in common an ambition to reap the benefits of administrative reform as an important means of expanding their policy power.

Nakasone's contribution

Although the process of administrative reform started in Japan in the 1960s, the rise of the prime ministerial executive really only began with the Nakasone administration in the mid-1980s. Prime Minister Tanaka Kakuei (1972–1974) was bent on forceful leadership and asserted his authority by using *ad hoc* mechanisms of executive coordination in crisis situations and by utilising the formal power resources that were available to their full potential,[31] but these still needed to be systematically developed and deployed to make them fully effective. In fact, Tanaka had to improvise given the lack of the necessary prime ministerial authority and a comprehensive institutional apparatus for the exercise of strong executive government led by the prime minister.[32]

Vigorously promoting administrative reform was without a doubt one of the top priorities of the Nakasone administration.[33] The prime minister openly admitted that one of his primary goals was to address 'the lack of power in the office of prime minister.'[34] In setting such a course, he moved quickly to continue the work on administrative reform that the cabinet of his predecessor, Prime Minister Suzuki Zenkō, had initiated under Nakasone's stewardship.[35] Significantly, the political strategies Nakasone used to bolster his power and promote top-down policymaking included 'creating power centers to counter the political parties and the bureaucracy by establishing many official and unofficial advisory councils. . . . [and] strengthening the Kantei by appointing more competent staff.'[36] Nakasone himself recalled,

I set up many councils to deal with the issue of administrative reform. I felt that it was necessary to scale down the size of government agencies and organizations that had grown excessively. . . . [reverse] the tendency toward centralization of state authority . . . [and abolish] restrictive, centralist control by an oversized bureaucracy.[37]

At the same time, he ordered his newly appointed, higher calibre personal secretaries to act as his assistants as well as his personal secretaries.[38]

Another of Nakasone's adept manoeuvres was to appoint as chief cabinet secretary Gotōda Masaharu whose administrative skills he needed to control the bureaucracy while he attempted administrative reform.[39] Moreover, Gotōda's connections with the Japanese police made corrupt politicians think twice before going against his wishes.[40] As Makihara writes, Nakasone

> chose bureaucrat-turned-politician Gotōda Masaharu, a former head of the National Police Agency known for his crisis-management and intelligence-gathering prowess. With Gotōda's help, he asserted the authority of the Cabinet Secretariat and its chief – and by extension, that of the prime minister – over the other . . . ministries and agencies.[41]

The Cabinet Secretariat underwent organisational changes that reinforced its capacity to support the prime minister in inter-ministry coordination with the formation of new cabinet councillor's offices – on external and internal affairs – and a cabinet security affairs office and cabinet information research office[42] known as the Cabinet Intelligence and Research Office. These were set up with the aim of encouraging the secretariat 'proactively to play a central role in dealing with matters that were difficult for the ministries and agencies to coordinate amongst themselves.'[43] Their specific purpose was to strengthen the Kantei,[44] which Nakasone saw as necessary to bolster his executive leadership,[45] and to concentrate executive authority.[46] Nakasone wanted strong staff support for the Kantei, which was separate from the bureaucracy, and which would serve the prime minister and enhance the central co-ordination mechanisms.[47] He keenly appreciated the fact that the key to greater prime ministerial power was the creation of an independent advisory and information-gathering structure dedicated to assisting the prime minister, which would act like a second bureaucracy and additional layer of bureaucratic machinery loyal to the prime minister and which would serve as the primary institutional means to boost prime ministerial power. In light of these developments, Nakasone's prime ministership marked the beginning of a trend towards 'a strong Kantei and a weak party (*kan kō tō tei*)'.[48]

Hashimoto's contribution

The process of central government reform took giant strides under the Hashimoto administration (*Hashimoto gyōkaku*), which established an Administrative Reform Council as an advisory body to the prime minister in 1996, which was chaired by Hashimoto himself.[49] The official purpose of the new council was to examine ways in which the functions of the prime minister and cabinet might be strengthened in order to enhance their input into the policymaking process.[50] The end goal was to create 'state governance based on the leadership of the cabinet, particularly the prime minister'.[51]

The council's final report of December 1997, which 'formed the core of the Basic Law on Central Government Reform',[52] stated that there was 'a need for "bold reinforcement of the functions of the Kantei and cabinet" in order to ensure that policy planning and policymaking were comprehensive and strategic.'[53] However, it was the Kantei, rather than the Kantei *and the cabinet*, which was strengthened by the reforms. Hashimoto himself was 'intent on Kantei leadership',[54] and so his administrative reforms established the necessary institutional structures for Kantei-led policymaking. He was the one who created a Kantei-centred political process,[55] making the prime ministerial executive rather than the formal political executive the primary beneficiary of central government reform.

The formal legal and institutional structures for such a system were implemented in January 2001 and included, firstly, expanding the prime minister's executive authority in relation to initiating policies.[56] Cabinet Law (*Naikakuhō*) was revised to grant the prime minister a clear legal right to propose important, basic policies as the chairman of cabinet meetings.[57] Previously, this right had not been specifically mentioned in Cabinet Law[58] but now enabled the prime minister to lead the decision-making process.[59] As Shinoda writes, 'With the revision of the Cabinet Law, institutional arrangements were clearly set for the national leader to initiate policies from the top.'[60]

Secondly, and even more importantly, the system that directly assisted the prime minister was transformed into a formidable policymaking infrastructure.[61] The range of functions, authority and staff of the Cabinet Secretariat were expanded, 'turning it into the administration's policymaking hub and buttressing the role of the chief cabinet secretary.'[62] It was a far cry from the tiny unit consisting of just the chief cabinet secretary and the prime minister's secretaries that had first been established in the early postwar period.[63] Moreover, existing Cabinet Law had only granted the Cabinet Secretariat the passive role of 'general coordination', but the revision added the more proactive roles of 'planning and proposing' important national policies.[64] This meant that the secretariat could now 'draft its own policies and even shut down objections from the ministries in the name of carrying out the basic policies of the prime minister and the cabinet.'[65] According to the wording of the official new 'Guidelines for the Policy Coordination System', the Cabinet Secretariat was empowered ' "to present policy direction for the government as a whole, and coordinate policy strategically and proactively". . . . [O]ther ministries [were instructed] to recognize that "the

Cabinet Secretariat is the highest and final organ for policy coordination under the Cabinet". This placed the Cabinet Secretariat above other ministries and agencies'[66] and positioned it 'as the brains behind Kantei leadership.'[67] It also buttressed the power of the prime minister in setting national policy, particularly vis-à-vis the bureaucracy. Designating the enlarged Cabinet Secretariat as the 'highest and final organ for policy coordination under the Cabinet. . . . strengthened the prime minister's power to coordinate policies among ministries',[68] with the prime minister also given the authority 'to fill key posts in the Cabinet Secretariat with officials from the various ministries and specialists from outside government.'[69] This avoided 'the previously rigid method of allocating particular posts to bureaucrats from specific ministries.'[70]

The powers of the chief cabinet secretary and deputy chief cabinet secretaries as leading officials in the government and as instruments of prime ministerial control were also significantly enhanced.[71] No longer did the chief cabinet secretary hold 'a relatively low-ranking cabinet position'.[72] Thereafter, this role became 'one of the most powerful positions in the Japanese government'[73] with the power to initiate policy planning. Previously, the chief cabinet secretary could only coordinate policymaking initiated by different parts of the bureaucracy.[74] As a result, the chief cabinet secretary became

> directly involved in the decision-making process for most of the government's important policy decisions. Even when the CCS [chief cabinet secretary] is not directly involved, he must vet decisions. It is no exaggeration to say that the CCS is much more involved than the prime minister in the policy-making process. The increasingly elevated status of the CCS symbolizes the emergence of the Kantei.[75]

Likewise, a parallel rise in the importance of the deputy chief cabinet secretaries elevated the administrative deputy chief cabinet secretary to 'a key position, often called the top post of the entire bureaucracy'[76] with the job of acting as 'liaison between the prime minister and the bureaucracy'.[77] Located in the Kantei with the chief cabinet secretary, the deputy chief cabinet secretaries primarily served the prime minister, not the cabinet, and were appointed by the prime minister in consultation with the cabinet.[78] As for the prime minister's own personal staff, he was newly empowered to appoint up to five special advisers (two more than previously) whose official role, under Cabinet Law, was to 'assist the prime minister'[79] and more than five private secretaries simply by issuing an executive order.[80]

The reforms also included the creation of a much more powerful Cabinet Office headed by the prime minister to replace the existing Prime Minister's

Office (Sōrifu).[81] Alongside the Cabinet Secretariat, units within the Sōrifu had previously provided administrative support to the prime minister who was assigned the Prime Minister's Office portfolio as 'first among equals' in the cabinet.[82] Unlike the Sōrifu, however, the new Cabinet Office was designed to act as a 'powerful support organ for the prime minister'[83] and to 'serve, in essence, as the administrative, coordinating, and research arm of the Cabinet Secretariat.'[84] Its several hundred staff, which, like the Cabinet Secretariat, were 'recruited from both the ministries and the private sector',[85] were placed under the direct authority of the prime minister and chief cabinet secretary.[86] They were tasked with planning and proposing policies and conducting general coordination in relation to important matters such as economic and fiscal policy, science and technology policy, disaster management and gender equality etc.[87] In elevating the Cabinet Office to the status of '"comprehensive coordinator" of interministerial affairs',[88] the reforms placed the office above the established ministries, simultaneously boosting its position in the bureaucratic hierarchy whilst subordinating the established ministries to the Kantei executive.

The combination of a reinforced Cabinet Secretariat and the establishment of the Cabinet Office vastly strengthened the institutional resource base supporting the prime minister in designing the basic direction of policies.[89] They now provided the prime minister with a mechanism for controlling and coordinating the activities of his government.[90] In furnishing such support, the administrative reforms were also an attempt to reduce the powers of the bureaucrats to initiate and formulate policies, in short to halt the 'bottom-up' policymaking process at its very beginning.

Also set up under the Cabinet Office were four new councils on important policies such as the CEFP, which Hashimoto designed, along with the Council for Science and Technology Policy and the Central Disaster Management Council etc.,[91] which were 'part of the formal policymaking process at the executive level.'[92] Their job was to 'investigate and deliberate key issues',[93] 'assist in "the planning and drafting, and comprehensive coordination needed for the integration of the policies of administrative branches"'[94] and 'become involved in policymaking at the macro level'.[95] Importantly, the councils were independent of the bureaucracy and were unconstrained by policy discussions in the bureaucracy and ruling party – effectively, a separate locus of policy deliberation on 'important cross-cutting national issues',[96] with powers to advise the prime minister on issues in their areas of jurisdiction. In addition to government ministers, they brought 'outsiders' into their discussions by drawing in representatives from the private sector, academe, labour unions etc.[97]

Chaired by the prime minister, the CEFP, for example, 'took charge of economic and fiscal policy'.[98] The fact that the prime minister chaired the council was particularly important, given that substantial discussions could be conducted and decisions could be made during council meetings, allowing the prime minister to exert significant influence over both the agenda and the conclusion of the discussions and enabling him to use the council 'to reflect his views in policies.'[99] Moreover, because all domestic policies were related in some way to the economy or fiscal matters, the council's remit expanded to include domestic policies in general.[100]

The CEFP also brought about other changes to the conventional patterns of policymaking. First, it reduced bureaucratic leadership over agenda-setting to a considerable extent. The private sector members of the council could suggest bold ideas that would never be suggested by either bureaucrats or *zoku*.[101] The council thus institutionalised a new route for introducing policy ideas into the policymaking process from outside the government, making it easier for the prime minister to tackle entrenched policies that protected vested interests. Secondly, the council opened up the policymaking process to other actors, which had previously been monopolised by closed policy subgovernments consisting of the ministries, *zoku* etc.[102] Thirdly, by having the prime minister, chief cabinet secretary and other major economic ministers as members of the council, it came to play a powerful 'agenda-integrating' function cutting across the vertically divided structure of policymaking centring on each of the ministries with their separate subgovernments and agendas. This set-up had traditionally prevented ministers and ministries having a say in matters that were officially within the jurisdiction of other ministries. Now the prime minister could more easily prioritise particular national policies as well as examine them for consistency.[103] He could also lead substantive discussions in the council amongst cabinet ministers, 'complementing cabinet meetings that had become ceremonial.'[104]

Another institutional prerogative bestowed on the prime minister by administrative reform was the right 'to create ministerial portfolios known as "minister of state for special missions"'[105] in the Cabinet Office with the official task of assisting the prime minister.[106] These posts were 'created to boost the prime minister's power to focus on high-value policy priorities'[107] and to 'support prime minister-led policymaking in the cabinet.'[108] Because the ministers of state were not bound by the standpoints of the established ministries, they could devote their efforts to promoting the prime minister's policy initiatives.[109] Instead, they were 'served by the various administrative components of the Cabinet Office.'[110] The new ministers in charge (of certain issues) were in the same position. Like the ministers of state for special missions, they did not control a ministry or agency but were ministers to assist the prime minister. Based on Article 12 of Cabinet Law, these positions were ministerial posts that the prime minister could establish in the Cabinet Secretariat. The two types of ministers also shared the characteristic of being responsible for general coordination (*sōgō chōsei*) duties unlike the ministers who were the heads of ministries.[111]

Taken together, the 2001 administrative reforms provided the prime minister with far greater capacity to 'coordinate, integrate and communicate'[112] his wishes on policy issues, particularly in those areas requiring a whole-of-government response. The impact of the reforms was further to shift the balance of policymaking power in the prime minister's favour by providing him with a much more formidable institutional resource base. Policymaking became more centralised and the prime minister could more easily exercise policy leadership.[113]

Although one of the major goals of the Hashimoto Administrative Reform Council was to strengthen both cabinet and prime ministerial authority, in reality, the effect of the administrative reforms was to strengthen the prime ministerial executive as a powerful new layer of government rather than the cabinet per se. As a result of the reforms, prime minister-centred policy-making became possible. Minister of State for Economic and Fiscal Policy in the Koizumi administration, Takenaka Heizō, later observed, 'During Hashimoto's administrative reforms in the late 1990s, reforms were carried out to the central ministries and agencies under the clear principles of "from bureaucratic leadership to political leadership" and "political leadership is the Kantei's leadership".'[114]

Administrative reform simultaneously weakened the ruling party and bureaucracy's role in policymaking as well as the alliance between ruling party members and ministry bureaucrats.[115] Assisting this shift was the transfer of some policymaking functions directly to staff who were under the supervision of the prime minister and who were not bureaucrats in individual ministries, thus making it easier for him to realise policy shifts.[116] The ministries could make claims about the need for continuity and consistency in policies but, as Machidori argues, it 'became much more difficult for them to use their veto against policy shifts.'[117]

Koizumi's contribution

Koizumi was the first Japanese leader to take full advantage of the Hashimoto reforms, which laid out a path for the Koizumi government to follow. The formal power resources now available to the prime minister to assert his policy leadership were put to good use, expanded and institutionalised.[118] In the Kantei itself, Koizumi benefited from a talented and dedicated team including unofficial advisers as well as Cabinet Secretariat staff.[119]

In terms of his direct relations with the bureaucracy, Koizumi relied on the strengthened Kantei to provide strong support for his policy direction. As Uchiyama reports, he 'emphasised the method whereby the prime minister and those close to him (chief cabinet secretary, deputy chief cabinet secretary etc.) gave clear instructions to the different ministries and agencies and made bureaucrats put the instructions into practice.'[120]

The most significant development, however, was Koizumi's deployment of the CEFP, launched in January 2001, almost four months before he became prime minister, as the 'Kantei's control tower',[121] the 'headquarters of Kantei-led economic policies',[122] the 'institutional core' of . . . [his] leadership on macro-economic policy'[123] and the 'main vehicle for structural reform and the primary locus of policy discussion and formulation by Koizumi's economic team'.[124] After Koizumi's first cabinet was inaugurated, he said, 'I am determined to make sufficient use of the cabinet's functions that were reinforced by the reforms to the central government ministries, for example by leading the Council on Economic and Fiscal Policy myself, and fulfil my responsibility as prime minister and leader of the cabinet'.[125] At the first meeting of the CEFP, he declared, 'It is not an exaggeration to say that this is the most important council in terms of fleshing out the major policy (for structural reform) that I included in my policy speech.'[126] With reform-minded Takenaka Heizō as Minister of State for Economic and Fiscal Policy,[127] the CEFP was able to provide the most important platform for Takenaka's policy input.[128] He was completely entrusted by Koizumi to perform the role of 'control tower' for structural reform and macroeconomic policy.[129] The principal sources of his power were Koizumi's complete trust in him and his skill in making full use of the CEFP, which was under Koizumi's direct control, as the 'main engine of reform'.[130] Takenaka reportedly took directions from Koizumi himself as chairman of the CEFP, while the council assumed responsibility for compiling the fiscal policy guidelines that shaped the broad outlines of the budget as well as played a vital role in formulating measures across a whole range of economic sectors, such as reforming the postal, financial and taxation systems.[131] Given the CEFP's assumption as a centralised, prime minister-directed policy organ, decisions on these matters were often made without discussion with or the agreement of the ruling party. As Uchiyama relates, Koizumi

> advanced policymaking through bodies such as the Council on Economic and Fiscal Policy etc. independently of the discussions in the LDP and made the party accept the result of the debate in the council. Furthermore, Koizumi consistently neglected the ruling party's screening system, which the *zoku giin* used as leverage to exercise influence.[132]

As a result, the CEFP and the LDP's Policy Affairs Research Council (PARC), which was 'the centre of the LDP's policy activities as the ruling party',[133] were often engaged in sharp conflict and continued to have a tense relationship from the time the Koizumi administration was inaugurated.[134] In fact, Koizumi's flouting of the convention of 'advance scrutiny' (*yotō shinsa*) and 'prior approval' (*jizen shōnin*) by the PARC (its policy divisions, research commissions and board) and the ruling party's Executive Council[135] became one of the main features of his Kantei leadership.[136] The custom was for the Executive Council first to get the PARC to examine matters before examining them itself, but Koizumi said, 'If people keep complaining we should just skip the PARC'.[137] He also 'changed the way Executive Council resolutions were made from being based on unanimous support to an actual vote'.[138] When it came to privatising postal services, which was the centrepiece of his reform efforts, Koizumi went even further, bypassing both the PARC and the Executive Council and submitting 'his postal reform bills directly to the Diet in the face of strong dissent against the bills within the LDP.'[139]

In his dealings with both his own party and the bureaucracy, it was quite clear that Koizumi wanted to discard the traditional bottom-up, consensus style of policy formation[140] and replace it with 'a top-down policymaking system based on "the leadership of the prime minister's Kantei [*shushō kantei shudō*]".'[141] Koizumi realised that the existing policymaking system could not deliver the reforms that he wanted. As Shimizu observes,

> The traditional 'double-headed eagle'-style policymaking mechanism where the Kantei and LDP stood side by side underwent change as Kantei leadership based on Koizumi's powerful leadership and the Council on Economic and Fiscal Policy led by the 'control tower' Takenaka significantly gained importance. The LDP's PARC, which was a stronghold of the vertically divided ministries and the *zoku giin*, has become dysfunctional, and the bottom-up system founded on the divisions has partially collapsed.[142]

In September 2002, 18 months after the inauguration of his administration, Koizumi revealed his determination to destroy the power of the *zoku giin*, especially in posts, roads and welfare, where they had the most power.[143] Although he listed only the 'big three', in reality five policy tribes traditionally exercised the most influence – posts, construction, welfare, agriculture and education – described as the 'five tribes under one union [*go zoku kyōwa*].'[144]

Koizumi was driven by the need to challenge the vested interests of the power structures that had hitherto dominated the policymaking process – namely the 'iron triangles' of bureaucrats, LDP policy tribes and associated interest groups.[145] Many of the structural reforms that his administration promoted involved cutting into these vested interests, such as reducing public works outlays, promoting deregulation and last, but not least, privatising the postal system.[146] In the face of strong opposition, previous administrations had avoided tackling these issues and, even if they did, were rarely able to make progress.[147] Koizumi realised that radical policy change that cut into the entrenched political and economic interests that had sustained the LDP regime over decades could not be accomplished without first changing the policymaking process itself. In short, 'Kantei leadership was a necessary condition for realising Koizumi's reforms.'[148]

In addition to 'Kantei leadership' (*kantei shudō*),[149] a variety of other terms were used to describe Koizumi's political style and policy impact including 'strong prime minister' (*tsuyoi shushō*),[150] 'Kantei-oriented politics (*kantei seiji*)',[151] 'Kantei-led policymaking',[152] 'prime ministerial rule' (*shushō shihai*)[153] and 'Kantei control' (*kantei shihai*).[154] These descriptions all reflected the reality of a decision-making process led by the Kantei and the fact that policy decisions that strongly reflected the prime minister's own intentions were being made.[155] Takenaka used the term 'prime ministerial rule' to describe Koizumi's administration, for example, in order to emphasise that the authority given to the prime minister by law had been strengthened and, at the same time, 'power had become concentrated in the prime minister'.[156] As Shimizu observes, 'There was no doubt that Kantei leadership dramatically strengthened under Koizumi. The striking individuality of Koizumi, who was fixated on the "prime ministership" and the new infrastructure that supported Kantei leadership had a synergistic effect that drastically strengthened their power.'[157]

Certainly, supporting personnel and policy structures such as the chief cabinet secretary, the Cabinet Secretariat, Cabinet Office and the CEFP were used as the primary machinery underpinning top-down decision-making by the prime minister.[158] Chief cabinet secretary in the Koizumi administration, Fukuda Yasuo, who emphasised the effect of Hashimoto's administrative reforms, said,

> People say that Koizumi is running off on his own, but he is working in accordance with the new systems formed after the reorganisation of the ministries and agencies, such as the prime minister's right to initiate important policies and the Council on Economic and Fiscal Policy. He is not going against any rules.[159]

Koizumi also developed the habit of handing ministers pieces of paper on which were written his specific instructions with respect to policies while, at the same time, encouraging ministers to debate policies in cabinet meetings in front of him before ultimately making the final decision.[160] As Mikuriya observes, 'Kantei leadership during Koizumi's days had the strong characteristic of being "Koizumi's leadership"'.[161]

However, Koizumi was not entirely successful in quelling opposition from counter-reform groups in his own party and in the bureaucracy to his policy initiatives and subordinating these resistance forces (*teikō seiryoku*) to the Kantei's executive authority.[162] Moreover, he was criticised for the relatively small 'arena' in which he demonstrated his policy leadership where he created scenes that looked like they had been taken from an action movie such as his theatrical advocacy of postal privatisation and his firing of Ministry of Posts and Telecommunications bureaucrats who objected.[163] Apart from certain key issues on which Koizumi had strong convictions such as postal privatisation and proactive support for the United States in Iraq in 2003, he 'literally left the decision-making to others such as then-Chief Cabinet Secretary Fukuda Yasuo and various cabinet members for other matters.'[164] When, for example, in December 2004, Koizumi met with LDP first-term Lower House members, he said, 'It is important to strike a balance between dictating and leaving decisions to others.'[165] In other words, 'Koizumi distinguished between policies that he himself decided and carried out, and policies that he delegated to cabinet members.'[166] As Mishima observes,

> [T]he prime ministership became an important source of new initiatives and functioned as a control tower overseeing policymaking. Of course, the old patterns of policymaking also remained. On issues in which Koizumi did not intervene, bilateral interactions between ministries and the zoku dominated policymaking, as in the past.[167]

There are limits, therefore, to the value of global generalisations about the nature of policymaking in the Koizumi administration from specific examples where Koizumi demonstrated executive power as prime minister.[168]

At the same time, as this analysis of the contributions of the Nakasone, Hashimoto and Koizumi administrations to administrative reform has shown, changes to central government policymaking procedures and processes, both those written into law and those initiated in an *ad hoc* fashion to complement formal-legal changes, including the rejection of unwritten policymaking conventions and traditions, were highly influential in the rise of the prime ministerial executive. Fundamentally, the process of administrative reform provided a whole new, substantial layer of policymaking to support the prime minister directly via the provision of support structures for supplying independent advice, expertise and information to the prime minister on policy matters. The effect was to furnish new mechanisms for initiating, directing and promoting policies that prime ministers wanted implemented.

By strengthening the organisational backing for the prime minister, administrative reform thus built a strong institutional base for prime ministerial policy leadership. Crucially, it also provided coordination mechanisms to help override bureaucratic sectionalism and the segregated domains of ruling party *zoku*, enabling prime ministers to formulate a 'whole of government' response to policy issues. In these various ways, administrative reform facilitated the emergence of a much more top-down policymaking process, challenging the traditional dominance of bureaucratic and ruling party actors and undermining the operations of subgovernments in particular policy domains. In short, administrative reform changed both the policymaking system and the distribution of power within it.

The contribution of electoral reform

Electoral reform was the major political reform that underpinned the rise of prime ministerial power by providing additional, formal and informal power resources, rather than formal institutional instruments, to assist the Japanese prime minister to exert his policy authority, particularly against his own party. The electoral reforms of 1996 are widely regarded as a contributory factor in the rise of prime ministerial power[169] by concentrating authority in the LDP in the party leader.[170] Because the prime minister is also the president of the ruling party, any factor that boosts his formal authority in the party concomitantly reinforces his standing and policy authority as leader of the government. As Takenaka argues, 'the first factor [that supports the prime minister's power] is the authority held by the LDP leader'.[171] There is no doubt that, in the case of the ruling LDP, electoral reform precipitated a distinct power shift in favour of the party president, and therefore the prime minister, by concentrating intra-party power in the hands of the party leader. As Uchiyama argues, 'The LDP's cohesion increased and possibilities for the prime minister to control general party members greatly expanded.'[172]

This was particularly the case in relation to other power centres in the party organisation itself. Electoral reform weakened the power of the LDP factions and particularly the faction heads in crucial areas such as electoral endorsement, political funding and the allocation of government and party posts. Indeed, the factions' most important function was that of distributing appointments,[173] with their influence over personnel affairs based on their powers relating to elections and political funds. These were undermined by electoral reform, which simultaneously generated incentives for ruling party Diet members to defer to the policy direction of their leader to whom all these powers had been transferred. In short, it centralised organisational authority within the party in the hands of its president. Koizumi was the first prime minister to disregard the factions and ignore the party's seniority system when appointing his cabinet members, which gave him leverage over his ministers.[174] After his appointment as LDP leader, he stated, 'I will not be caught up in factions. The factions will not submit a list of members, and they have said that they will not make any requests. My first job is to show that the order in the party has changed in terms of personnel affairs.'[175] Two days later when Koizumi was appointed prime minister 'he went on to make personnel decisions for cabinet members. Koizumi himself described the decisions as "earth shattering".'[176]

Electoral reform also meant that there was more emphasis on the prime minister as party leader, giving him a higher public profile both in elections and as the leader of the government. Under the changed electoral system, candidates in single-member districts could no longer rely solely on personal votes so their party identification became more important as did the public image of the party leader.[177] At election time, the prime minister became the most prominent public face of his party and promoter of its policy manifesto,[178] thus strengthening his legitimacy as a choice based on public opinion and voters' electoral preferences. It meant that, after electoral reform, voters chose administrations and their prime ministers, who were given a mandate from the voters through the election.[179]

These same political realities also ensured that once in office, the prime minister acted as the government's main public relations officer via the media, explaining and justifying government policies to the public.[180] In these circumstances, a greater premium came to be placed on party presidents and prime ministers who offered strong policy leadership, who could attract voters and who were effective communicators on a public level.[181] As Takenaka argues,

> The conditions that need to be fulfilled to obtain and maintain the post of prime minister changed. . . . Winning the support of public opinion became a necessary condition for obtaining and maintaining the post of prime minister and the process by which the prime minister's power became strengthened.[182]

It also meant that party leaders who were popular amongst the voting public were more effective in stabilising their support base amongst their party's rank and file Diet members because the latter's electoral fate hinged to a greater degree on the popularity of their leader. Election candidates became more conscious of how the image of the leader either helped or hindered their campaigns. Prime ministers could turn this to their advantage in the policymaking process if they retained high levels of public backing.[183] In other words, the prime minister's public standing could be used to assist him in pursuing not only victories for himself and fellow candidates in general elections but also in acting as a support base in policy battles that he might have with others in his own party. A strong public support base also acted as a disincentive for Diet members of the ruling party to mobilise against the prime minister and his office on policy and other matters, given that their electoral fate was more strongly linked to that of their leader.

In this way, electoral reform created opportunities for prime ministers to build a support base *outside the party* by appealing directly to the electorate. They could then use the power of public opinion to counter intra-party opposition to policy initiatives emanating from the Kantei. In these kinds of political situations, strong public backing could become a decisive factor working in favour of the prime minister even against his own party. It was Koizumi who used the populist support card most strongly against the so-called 'resistance forces' in the LDP. As Mishima points out, 'His high level of grassroots popularity was a vital political resource in the fight against opponents within his party.'[184] Takenaka described Koizumi's administration as 'prime ministerial rule' not only because the authority that the law gave to the prime minister had strengthened but also because the prime minister's authority as ruling party leader had been augmented 'against the backdrop of winning the support of public opinion.'[185] Both the political and administrative reforms enacted in the 1990s thus produced results during the Koizumi administration.[186]

To sum up, when comparing the contribution of administrative and electoral reforms to the rise of the prime ministerial executive, it is clear that the role of administrative reform was pivotal, with prime ministers who were bent on aggrandising their policymaking authority playing a crucial part in pushing the process along and exploiting the potential that the institutional changes offered. This prime minister-sponsored, proactive reform process became the strongest force for modernising Japan's political system. At the same time, while electoral reform did not create the institutional means to support, generate and augment prime ministerial power, it did buttress the authority of the party leader and prime minister *within the ruling party*, which indirectly assisted the exercise of his influence over policy and that of his executive office. The processes of electoral and central government reform were, therefore, mutually reinforcing. As Krauss and Pekkanen point out, it was the combination of 'fundamental structural changes that had taken place in the electorate, the LDP, and the government that . . . increased the potential for a stronger, more centralized political leadership.'[187]

Notes

1 See, for example, Angel, Robert C., 'Prime Ministerial Leadership in Japan: Recent Changes in Personal Style and Administrative Organization', *Pacific Affairs*, Vol. 61, No. 4, Winter 1988–1989, pp. 583–602; Krauss, Ellis S. and Nyblade, Benjamin, '"Presidentialization" in Japan? The Prime Minister, Media and Elections in Japan', *British Journal of Political Science*, Vol. 35, No. 2,

April 2005, pp. 357–368; Machidori, Satoshi, *Shushō seiji no seido bunseki: Gendai Nihon seiji no kenryoku kiban keisei* [*The Japanese Premiership: An Institutional Analysis of the Power Relations*], Tokyo, Chikura Shobō, 2012, p. 68.

2 See, for example, Angel, 'Prime Ministerial Leadership in Japan', pp. 583, 588; Uchiyama, Yū, *Koizumi and Japanese Politics: Reform Strategies and Leadership Style*, Trans. Carl Freire, New York and London, Routledge, 2010, p. 126.

3 Uchiyama, *Koizumi and Japanese Politics*, p. 126.

4 See, for example, Hayao, Kenji, *The Japanese Prime Minister and Public Policy*, Pittsburgh, PA, University of Pittsburgh Press, 1993, pp. 27, 201; Richardson, Bradley, *Japanese Democracy. Power, Coordination, and Performance*, New Haven, CT, Yale University Press, 1997, p. 105; Stockwin, J.A.A., *Governing Japan: Divided Politics in a Major Economy*, 3rd edn. Oxford, Blackwell, 1999, p. 97, Shinoda, Tomohito, *Leading Japan: The Role of the Prime Minister*, Westport, Praeger, 2000; Masuyama, Mikitaka and Nyblade, Benjamin, 'Japan: The Prime Minister and the Japanese Diet', *The Journal of Legislative Studies*, Vol. 10, No. 2/3, Summer/Autumn 2004, pp. 250–262; Krauss and Nyblade, '"Presidentialization" in Japan?', p. 357; Takayasu, Kensuke, 'Prime-ministerial Power in Japan: A Re-Examination', *Japan Forum*, Vol. 17, No. 2, 2005, p. 163; Nyblade, Benjamin, 'The 21st Century Japanese Prime Minister: An Unusually Precarious Perch', *Journal of Social Science*, Vol. 61, No. 2, February 2011, p. 196.

5 Masuyama and Nyblade, 'Japan: The Prime Minister', p. 259.

6 *Blueprint for a New Japan*, p. 25.

7 *Blueprint for a New Japan*, p. 24.

8 Hayao, *The Japanese Prime Minister*, p. 18.

9 The male pronoun 'he' is used because all Japanese prime ministers have so far been male.

10 Richardson, *Japanese Democracy*, p. 105.

11 Krauss and Nyblade, '"Presidentialization" in Japan?', p. 358.

12 George, Aurelia, *An Overview of Japanese Politics*, Paper presented to the Japanese Economic and Management Studies Centre, University of New South Wales 'Understanding Japan Today' series, 3 November 1992, p. 3.

13 Uchiyama, *Koizumi and Japanese Politics*, p. 129.

14 Van Wolferen, Karel, *The Enigma of Japanese Power*, New York, Vintage Books, 1990, pp. 5–6.

15 Fukai, Shigeko N., 'The Missing Leader: The Structure and Traits of Political Leadership in Japan', in Ofer Feldman (ed.), *Political Psychology in Japan*, Nova Science Publishers, Inc., Commack, New York, 1998, p. 173.

16 Ozawa, *Blueprint for a New Japan*, p. 24.

17 See George Mulgan, Aurelia, 'Where Tradition Meets Change: Japan's Agricultural Politics in Transition', *Journal of Japanese Studies*, Vol. 31, No. 2, Summer 2005, pp. 261–298; George Mulgan, Aurelia, 'The Politics of Economic Reform', in Alisa Gaunder (ed.), *Handbook of Japanese Politics*, Abingdon and New York, Routledge, 2011, pp. 261–272; George Mulgan, Aurelia, "Agriculture", in James Babb (ed.), *Handbook of Modern Japanese Studies*, Sage, Thousand Oaks, CA, 2015, pp. 737–761.

18 As Shimizu argues, 'The mutually dependent relationship amongst the tribe Diet members, government offices and industries became the foundation of the triangle amongst politicians, bureaucrats and industries.' Shimizu,

Masato, *Kantei shudō: Koizumi Junichirō no kakumei* [*Kantei Leadership: The Revolution of Koizumi Junichirō*], Tokyo, Nihon Keizai Shinbunsha, 2005, p. 365.

19 See, for example, Iio, Jun, *Nihon no tōchi kōzō: Kanryō naikakusei kara giin naikakusei e* [*Japan's Structure of Governance: From a Bureaucratic to a Parliamentary Cabinet System*], Tokyo, Chūō Kōron Shinsha, 2007, p. 96 *et passim*; Uchiyama, 'Nihon seiji no akutā', p. 10; George Mulgan, Aurelia, 'Loosening the Ties That Bind: Japan's Agricultural Policy Triangle and Reform of Cooperatives (JA)', *Journal of Japanese Studies*, Vol. 42, No. 2, Summer 2016, p. 221.

20 George Mulgan, Aurelia, 'Japan's "Un-Westminster" System: Impediments to Reform in a Crisis Economy', *Government and Opposition*, Vol. 38, No. 1, January 2003, pp. 73–91.

21 Katō, Hideki, 'Political Reform of the Japanese System of Government (Symposium Report 2), *Tokyo Foundation*, 28 October 2008, www.tokyofoundation. org/en/articles/2008/political-reform-of-the-japanese-system-of-government-symposium-report-2.

22 Katō, 'Political Reform', www.tokyofoundation.org/en/articles/2008/political-reform-of-the-japanese-system-of-government-symposium-report-2.

23 See, for example, George Mulgan, Aurelia, *Japan's Failed Revolution: Koizumi and the Politics of Economic Reform*, Canberra, ANU Press, 2002, pp. 129–176.

24 This is somewhat different from Takenaka's argument that the dominant trend in Japanese politics has been characterised by the centralisation of power in the prime minister, namely 'rule by the Prime Minister'. Sakano, Tomokazu, *The Presidentialization of Politics in Britain and Japan: Comparing Party Responses to Electoral Dealignment*, Paper presented at the 2006 IPSA World Congress, Fukuoka, Japan, 10–14 July 2006, p. 21, quoting the title of the book by Takenaka, Harukata, *Shushō shihai: Nihon seiji no henbō* [*Prime Ministerial Rule: The Transformation of Japanese Politics*], Tokyo, Chūō Kōron Shinsha, 2006. See also below.

25 Makihara, Izuru, 'Seisaku kettei ni okeru shushō kantei no yakuwari' ['The Role of the Kantei in Making Policy'], *Nippon.com*, 27 June 2013, www. nippon.com/ja/features/c00408/.

26 As Mikuriya writes, 'After Nakasone, [prime ministers] have always been aiming to become strong prime ministers (*tsuyoi shushō*). Hashimoto and Koizumi were the same (they were aiming to become strong prime ministers too).' *Abe seiken wa hontō ni tsuyoi no ka* [*Is the Abe Administration Actually Strong?*], Tokyo, PHP Kenkyūjo, 2015, p. 129. Machidori identifies Nakasone and Koizumi as 'the two most notable prime ministers' in post-war Japanese politics, given their five-year tenures, and argues that these two leaders were exceptions to the norm of 'weak prime ministers'. *Shushō seiji*, pp. 67, 68. See also Krauss, Ellis S. and Pekkanen, Robert J., *The Rise and Fall of Japan's LDP: Political Party Organizations as Historical Institutions*, Ithaca, NY, Cornell University Press, 2010, pp. 220–224.

27 Nakasone, Yasuhiro, 'Pitchers and Catchers: Politicians, Bureaucrats, and Policy-Making in Japan', *Asia-Pacific Review*, Vol. 2, No. 1, 1995, p. 7.

28 Mikuriya, *Abe seiken*, p. 175.

29 Mikuriya, *Abe seiken*, p. 175.

30 Machidori, *Shushō seiji*, p. 94.

31 Takayasu, 'Prime-ministerial Power in Japan', pp. 170–178.

32 Woodall writes that both Tanaka and Nakasone 'displayed the sort of personal leadership that might be construed as prime ministerial government'. Woodall,

Brian, *Growing Democracy in Japan: The Parliamentary Cabinet System Since 1868*, Lexington, University Press of Kentucky, 2014, p. 155. 'Prime ministerial government' is defined by Dunleavy and Rhodes as being characterised by 'a generalized ability to decide policy across all issue areas in which he or she takes an interest' and 'by defining a governing "ethos," "atmosphere," or operating ideology which generates predictable and determinate solutions to most policy problems'. 'Core Executive Studies in Britain', *Public Administration*, Vol. 68, 1990, pp. 5, 8, quoted in Woodall, *Growing Democracy*, p. 155.

33 Liberal Democratic Party of Japan, 'Chapter Eleven, Period of President Nakasone's Leadership', *A History of the Liberal Democratic Party*, www.jimin.jp/english/about-ldp/history/104291.html.

34 Nakasone, 'Pitchers and Catchers', p. 8.

35 Liberal Democratic Party of Japan, 'Chapter Eleven', www.jimin.jp/english/about-ldp/history/104291.html. As Stockwin also reminds us, Nakasone was Director of the Administrative Management Agency between 1980 and 1982 (during Suzuki's prime ministership), and he used it to launch the Second Ad Hoc Administrative Reform Commission, which reported during his prime ministership. Stockwin, J.A.A., *Dictionary of the Modern Politics of Japan*, London and New York, Routledge, 2003, p. 2.

36 Shinoda, Tomohito, *Koizumi Diplomacy: Japan's Kantei Approach to Foreign and Defense Affairs*, Seattle and London, University of Washington Press, 2007, p. 26.

37 Nakasone, 'Pitchers and Catchers', p. 8.

38 Shinoda, *Koizumi Diplomacy*, p. 27.

39 Shinoda, *Koizumi Diplomacy*, p. 27.

40 Professor Brian Woodall, personal communication, 27 October 2016.

41 Makihara, 'The Role of the Kantei in Making Policy', *Nippon.com*, 7 August 2013, www.nippon.com/en/features/c00408/.

42 Takayasu, 'Prime-ministerial Power in Japan', p. 165.

43 Iio, *Nihon no tōchi kōzō*, pp. 62–63. Shinoda reports that Gotōda established five offices in the Kantei under the Cabinet Secretariat, which he calls 'cabinet offices': the Cabinet Office on Internal Affairs, the Cabinet Office on External Affairs, the Cabinet Office on Security Affairs, the Cabinet Public Affairs Office and the Cabinet Information and Research Office'. *Koizumi Diplomacy*, pp. 33–37.

44 Shinoda, *Koizumi Diplomacy*, p. 70.

45 Makihara, 'The Role of the Kantei in Making Policy', www.nippon.com/en/features/c00408/.

46 Mochizuki, Mike M., 'Japan's Long Transition: The Politics of Recalibrating Grand Strategy', in Ashley J. Tellis and Michael Wills (eds), *Domestic Political Change and Grand Strategy, Strategic Asia 2007–08*, Seattle, The National Bureau of Asian Research, 2007, p. 85.

47 Takayasu, 'Prime-ministerial Power in Japan', p. 165.

48 Mikuriya, *Abe seiken*, p. 42.

49 Connors, Lesley, 'Next Steps for Japan: Administrative Reform and the Changing Policy', *Asia-Pacific Review*, Vol. 7, No. 1, 2000, p. 114.

50 Connors, 'Next Steps for Japan', p. 114.

51 Machidori, *Shushō seiji*, p. 57.

52 Connors, 'Next Steps for Japan', p. 114.

53 Machidori, *Shushō seiji*, p. 57.

54 Shimizu, *Kantei shudō*, p. 226.
55 Curtis, for example, argues that Hashimoto 'initiated the administrative reforms that have created this prime minister centered political process'. Curtis, Gerald L., *Japan Update Speech*, Paper delivered to the Japan Update Conference, Crawford School, Australian National University, Canberra, 21st September 2016, p. 6.
56 Takenaka, *Shushō shihai*, p. 5.
57 Takenaka, *Shushō shihai*, pp. 158.
58 Uchiyama, 'Nihon seiji no akutā', p. 12.
59 Machidori, *Shushō seiji*, p. 173.
60 'Stronger Political Leadership in Japan', p. 105. See also Shinoda, *Koizumi Diplomacy*, p. 77, where he writes, 'With this revision, institutional arrangements were clearly set for the national leader to initiate policies at the top.'
61 Uchiyama, 'Nihon seiji no akutā', p. 12.
62 Makihara, Izuru, 'Abe's Enforcer: Suga Yoshihide's Stabilizing Influence on the Cabinet', *Nippon.com*, 25 September 2014, www.nippon.com/en/currents/d00135/.
63 Makihara, 'Seisaku kettei', www.nippon.com/ja/features/c00408/.
64 Uchiyama, 'Nihon seiji no akutā', p. 12. Article 12, Clause 2(3) of the Cabinet Law states that the 'administrative matters under the jurisdiction of the Cabinet Secretariat' involve '[p]lanning and proposing and administrative affairs relating to general coordination pertaining to important policies in the cabinet and important items in cabinet meetings.' Several other clauses in the same article also repeat the phrase 'planning and proposing and coordinating' in relation to other matters. *Naikakuhō [Cabinet Law]*, http://law.e-gov.go.jp/htmldata/S22/S22HO005.html.
65 Makihara, 'The Role of the Kantei in Making Policy', www.nippon.com/en/features/c00408/.
66 Shinoda, Tomohito, 'Stronger Political Leadership and the Shift in Policy-making Boundaries in Japan', in Glenn D. Hook (ed.) *Decoding Boundaries in Contemporary Japan: The Koizumi Administration and Beyond*, London and New York, Routledge, 2011, p. 105. See also Shinoda, Tomohito, 'Koizumi's Top-Down Leadership in the Anti-Terrorism Legislation: the Impact of Political Institutional Changes', *SAIS Review 23*, No. 1, Winter/Spring 2003, pp. 25–26; Shinoda, Tomohito, 'Japan's Cabinet Secretariat and Its Emergence as Core Executive', *Asian Survey*, Vol. 45, No. 5, 2005, p. 813; Shinoda, *Koizumi Diplomacy*, p. 77; Shinoda, Tomohito, 'Prime Ministerial Leadership', in Alisa Gaunder (ed.), *The Routledge Handbook of Japanese Politics*, London and New York, Routledge, 2011, p. 57.
67 Shimizu, *Kantei shudō*, p. 227.
68 Shinoda, 'Prime Ministerial Leadership', p. 57.
69 Woodall, *Growing Democracy*, p. 177.
70 Shinoda, 'Japan's Cabinet Secretariat', p. 807.
71 Shinoda, 'Japan's Cabinet Secretariat', p. 807; Estevez-Abe, Margarita, Hikotani, Takako and Nagahisa, Toshio, 'Japan's New Executive Leadership: How Electoral Rules Make Japanese Security Policy', in Masaru Kohno and Frances Rosenbluth (eds), *Japan and the World: Japan's Contemporary Geopolitical Challenges*, New Haven, CT, Yale CEAS Occasional Publications, Volume 2, 2008, p. 270.
72 Mochizuki, 'Japan's Long Transition', p. 85.

73 Mochizuki, 'Japan's Long Transition', p. 85.
74 Kaihara, Hiroshi, 'The Advent of a New Japanese Politics: Effects of the 1994 Revision of the Electoral Law', *Asian Survey*, Vol. 47, No. 5, 2007, p. 753.
75 Shinoda, *Koizumi Diplomacy*, p. 65. See also 'Japan's Cabinet Secretariat', p. 802, where he writes, the CCS's role is to be 'directly involved in the decision-making process for most of the government's key policy decisions. . . . It is not too much to say that the CCS is much more involved in policy-making than the prime minister'.
76 Shinoda, 'Japan's Cabinet Secretariat', pp. 803–804.
77 Shinoda, 'Japan's Cabinet Secretariat', pp. 803–804.
78 Report Memorandum #01–02, *Central Government Reform in Japan*, www.nsf.gov/od/oise/tokyo/reports/trm/rm01-02.html.
79 Tazaki, Shirō, *Abe kantei no shōtai* [*The Truth about Abe's Kantei*], Tokyo, Kōdansha, 2014, p. 53.
80 Shinoda, *Koizumi Diplomacy*, p. 70; Shinoda, 'Prime Ministerial Leadership', p. 57; Shinoda, 'Stronger Political Leadership', p. 105. See also Woodall, *Growing Democracy*, p. 177.
81 George Mulgan, 'Japan's "Un-Westminster" System', pp. 87–88. See also Sakano, *The Presidentialization of Politics*, p. 15, where he writes,

> The administrative reforms of January 2001 included the creation of a much more powerful Cabinet Office (Naikakufu) to replace the former Sorifu.' The Sōrifu was established by legislation in 1949, which later underwent extensive amendment. Maki noted 'the growth, particularly since 1952, of executive power, especially under the Prime Minister's Office (PMO), a special executive organ of the cabinet set up under the direct control of the prime minister . . . can also directly influence policy and its execution.'

Maki, John M., 'Executive Power in Japan', *Far Eastern Survey*, Vol. 24, No. 5, May 1955, p. 71. He argued that this development was particularly salient during the prime ministership of Yoshida Shigeru in 1948–1954.
82 Makihara, 'Seisaku kettei', www.nippon.com/ja/features/c00408/.
83 Shinoda, 'Prime Ministerial Leadership', in Gaunder, p. 56.
84 Report Memorandum #01–02, *Central Government Reform in Japan*, www.nsf.gov/od/oise/tokyo/reports/trm/rm01-02.html.
85 Report Memorandum #01–02, *Central Government Reform in Japan*, www.nsf.gov/od/oise/tokyo/reports/trm/rm01-02.html.
86 Woodall, *Growing Democracy*, p. 176.
87 Uchiyama, 'Nihon seiji no akutā', p. 12. The Law for Establishment of the Cabinet Office (*Naikakufu Setchihō*) lists these functions and the specific policy matters under the jurisdiction of the Cabinet Office, which run the gamut of national policy.
88 Woodall, *Growing Democracy*, p. 178.
89 Uchiyama, 'Nihon seiji no akutā', p. 12; Machidori, *Shushō seiji*, p. 90.
90 Report Memorandum #01–02, *Central Government Reform in Japan*, www.nsf.gov/od/oise/tokyo/reports/trm/rm01-02.html.
91 The fourth was the Council for Gender Equality. Their number later rose to the current five.
92 George Mulgan, *Japan's Failed Revolution*, p. 77.
93 Uchiyama, 'Nihon seiji no akutā', p. 12.
94 Woodall, *Growing Democracy*, p. 176.

95   Machidori, *Shushō seiji*, p. 57.
96   Report Memorandum #01–02, *Central Government Reform in Japan*, www. nsf.gov/od/oise/tokyo/reports/trm/rm01-02.html.
97   Woodall, *Growing Democracy*, p. 176.
98   Takayasu, 'Prime-ministerial Power in Japan', p. 180, fn 4.
99   Takenaka, *Shushō shihai*, pp. 5, 160.
100 Takenaka, *Shushō shihai*, p. 159.
101 Uchiyama, 'Nihon seiji no akutā', p. 13.
102 Uchiyama, 'Nihon seiji no akutā', p. 13.
103 Uchiyama, 'Nihon seiji no akutā', p. 13.
104 Uchiyama, 'Nihon seiji no akutā', p. 13.
105 Woodall, *Growing Democracy*, p. 9.
106 The ministers of state for special missions are based on Article 9 of the Law for the Establishment of the Cabinet Office, which states that the prime minister can establish posts that assist the prime minister.
107 Woodall, *Growing Democracy*, p. 177.
108 Uchiyama, 'Nihon seiji no akutā', p. 12.
109 Uchiyama, 'Nihon seiji no akutā', p. 12.
110 George Mulgan, *Japan's Failed Revolution*, p. 74.
111 'Dai 189 kai kokkai naikaku iinkai dai 23 gō' ['189th Diet Session Cabinet Committee No.23'], *Diet website*, 3 September 2015, http://kokkai.ndl.go.jp/SENTAKU/sangiin/189/0058/18909030058023a.html.
112 Takayasu, 'The Pressures of Change', www.nippon.com/en/features/c00410/.
113 Shinoda, 'Core Executive', pp. 820–821.
114 Takenaka, Heizō, 'Abe seiken no seisaku kettei purosesu' ['The Abe Administration's Policymaking Process'], *Japan Center for Economic Research* (An article for the series "Takenaka Heizō no Porishī Sukūru" ["Heizō Takenaka's Policy School"]), 26 November 2013, www.jcer.or.jp/column/takenaka/index565.html.
115 Machidori, *Shushō seiji*, p. 91.
116 Machidori, *Shushō seiji*, p. 91.
117 Machidori, *Shushō seiji*, p. 90.
118 George Mulgan, *Japan's Failed Revolution*, pp. 73–95; Sakano, *The Presidentialization of Politics*, p. 15. As Maclachlan argues, 'Koizumi and his team of reformers took advantage of new institutional opportunities to create a top-down system of executive leadership'. Maclachlan, Patricia, *The People's Post Office: The History and Politics of the Japanese Postal System, 1871–2010*, Cambridge, MA, Harvard University Press, 2012, p. 18.
119 Makihara, 'The Role of the Kantei in Making Policy', www.nippon.com/en/features/c00408/.
120 Uchiyama, 'Nihon seiji no akutā', p. 10. However, Mishima argues that 'Koizumi was utterly unsuccessful in checking bureaucratic influence' and 'the strong position of the bureaucracy basically remained intact even under his cabinet'. Mishima, Ko, 'Grading Japanese Prime Minister Koizumi's Revolution', *Asian Survey*, Vol. 47, No. 5, 2007, pp. 731, 747.
121 Shimizu, *Kantei shudō*, p. 247. Shimizu also called the Cabinet Secretariat and Takenaka Heizo the 'control tower' of Koizumi's administration. See also below.
122 Asano, Takaaki, 'Abenomikusu o sasaeru mittsu no seisaku kaigi' ['The Three Policy Councils that Support Abenomics'], *The Tokyo Foundation*, 2 July 2013

(Reproduced from *Bijinesu Hōmu*, July 2013 edition), www.tkfd.or.jp/research/project/news.php?id=1158.
123 Machidori, *Shushō seiji*, p. 99.
124 George Mulgan, *Japan's Failed Revolution*, p. 74.
125 Takenaka, *Shushō shihai*, p. 160.
126 Shimizu, *Kantei shudō*, p. 246.
127 Mishima, 'Grading Japanese Prime Minister Koizumi's Revolution', p. 731.
128 George Mulgan, *Japan's Failed Revolution*, p. 79.
129 Shimizu, *Kantei shudō*, p. 214.
130 Shimizu, Masato, *Keizai zaisei senki – Kantei shudō Koizumi kara Abe e* [*History of the Economic and Fiscal War – Kantei Leadership, from Koizumi to Abe*], Tokyo, Nihon Keizai Shinbun Shuppansha, 2007, p. 48.
131 Estevez-Abe, Hikotani and Nagahisa, 'Japan's New Executive Leadership', p. 276.
132 Uchiyama, 'Nihon seiji no akutā', p. 11.
133 Iio, *Nihon no tōchi kōzō*, p. 83.
134 Shimizu, *Kantei shudō*, p. 9. Curtis observed at the time that,

> Since Koizumi has come into office, a virtual dual-power structure has emerged between the prime minister's office, the kantei, and the LDP, with the head of the executive council and the policy affairs research council regularly opposing the policies of the prime minister.

Curtis, Gerald L., *Institutional Change and Political Reform: Back to Basics*, Discussion Paper No. 33, Discussion Paper Series, APEC Study Center, Columbia Business School, September 2004, pp. 6–7. It was a case of 'the prime minister versus the ruling camp'. George Mulgan, *Japan's Failed Revolution*, p. 193, citing the *Mainichi Shinbun*, 24 July 2002.
135 The Executive Council's decision is crucial because, as Iio explains, its

> decision is adopted as the LDP's decision . . . [and] all LDP members . . . are subjected to 'compulsory adherence to the party line [*tōgi kōsoku*]'. . . . [T]his guarantees . . . that . . . Diet members belonging to the party will automatically support the bill submitted by the government'. . . . [W]hat is of great importance is that the cabinet does not approve bills that do not go through the ruling party's prior screening system.

Nihon no tōchi kōzō, p. 87.
136 Machidori, *Shushō seiji*, p. 99. Here, Machidori was referring to the argument of Ōtake Hideo, *Koizumi Junichirō popyurizumu no kenkyū* [*A Study of Koizumi Junichirō's Populism*], Tokyo, Tōyō Keizai Shinpōsha, 2006, p. 96, which argued, 'mainly in relation to macroeconomic management, "the function of the Council on Economic and Fiscal Policy chaired by the prime minister as the institutional core and Koizumi's forcible methods that ignored the custom of prior screening by the LDP's PARC and Executive Council were the two main aspects" of "Kantei leadership".'
137 Mikuriya, *Abe seiken*, p. 182.
138 Mikuriya, *Abe seiken*, p. 184.
139 Sakano, *The Presidentialization of Politics*, p. 16.
140 Estevez-Abe, Hikotani and Nagahisa, 'Japan's New Executive Leadership', p. 277.
141 Uchiyama, 'Nihon seiji no akutā', p. 10.

142 Shimizu, *Kantei Shudō*, p. 301.
143 Shimizu, *Kantei shudō*, p. 363.
144 Shimizu, *Kantei shudō*, p. 365.
145 Uchiyama, 'Nihon seiji no akutā', p. 10.
146 Uchiyama, 'Nihon seiji no akutā', p. 10.
147 Uchiyama, 'Nihon seiji no akutā', p. 10.
148 Uchiyama, 'Nihon seiji no akutā', p. 10.
149 Mikuriya, *Abe seiken*, p. 42.
150 Machidori, *Shushō seiji*, p. 99, referring to the term used by Kamikawa Ryūnoshin, in his book *Koizumi Kaikaku no Seijigaku* [*The Political Science of Koizumi's Reforms*], Tokyo, Tōyō Keizai Shinpōsha, 2010.
151 Sugiura Nobuhiko, *JA ga kawareba Nihon no nōgyō wa tsuyoku naru* [*Japan's Agricultural Industry Will Become Stronger If JA Changes*], Tokyo, Discover21, 2015, p. 29.
152 According to Shinoda, the phrase 'Kantei-led policymaking' frequently appeared in the media during Koizumi's term of office. *Koizumi Diplomacy*, p. 9.
153 See, for example, Takenaka, *Shushō shihai*.
154 Mikuriya, *Abe seiken*, p. 42.
155 Machidori, *Shushō seiji*, p. 99 quoting Kamikawa, *Koizumi Kaikaku no Seijigaku.*
156 Machidori, *Shushō seiji*, p. 99, referring to Takenaka's analysis in *Shushō shihai*, pp. 4–7.
157 Shimizu, *Kantei shudō*, p. 369.
158 Sakano, *The Presidentialization of Politics*, p. 16.
159 Quoted in Shimizu, *Kantei shudō*, p. 369.
160 Iio, *Nihon no tōchi kōzō*, p. 196.
161 Mikuriya, *Abe seiken*, p. 42.
162 George Mulgan, *Japan's Failed Revolution*; George Mulgan, 'Where Tradition Meets Change', pp. 261–298; Mishima, 'Grading Japanese Prime Minister Koizumi's Revolution', pp. 727–748; George Mulgan, 'The Politics of Economic Reform', p. 262; Woodall, for example, writes, 'Although the government bureaucracy had lost much of its luster, it remained a force in executive affairs.' *Growing Democracy*, p. 177.
163 Mikuriya, *Abe seiken*, p. 42.
164 Tazaki, *Abe kantei*, p. 66.
165 Tazaki, *Abe kantei*, p. 39.
166 Tazaki, *Abe kantei*, p. 39.
167 Mishima, 'Grading Japanese Prime Minister Koizumi's Revolution', p. 730.
168 See, for example, Takenaka, *Shushō shihai*; Noble, Gregory W., 'Seijiteki rīdāshippu to kōzō kaikaku' ['Political Leadership and Structural Reform'], in Tōkyō Daigaku Shakai Kagaku Kenkyūjo (eds), *Ushinawareta 10 nen o koete (II) Koizumi kaikaku no jidai e* [*Beyond the Lost Decade (II) Toward the Age of Koizumi Reform*], Tokyo, Tōkyō Daigaku Shuppankai, 2006; Shinoda, *Koizumi Diplomacy*.
169 Takenaka, *Shushō shihai*, p. 158; Estevez-Abe, Hikotani and Nagahisa, 'Japan's New Executive Leadership', p. 252, 254; Uchiyama, 'Nihon seiji no akutā', p. 11; Machidori, *Shushō seiji*, p. 58.
170 Uchiyama, 'Nihon seiji no akutā', p. 11.
171 Takenaka, *Shushō shihai*, p. 5.
172 Uchiyama, 'Nihon seiji no akutā', p. 12.
173 Uchiyama, *Koizumi and Japanese Politics*, p. 13.

174 Uchiyama, 'Nihon seiji no akutā', p. 13.
175 Takenaka, *Shushō shihai*, p. 156.
176 Takenaka, *Shushō shihai*, p. 157.
177 Krauss and Pekkanen, *The Rise and Fall of Japan's LDP*, pp. 235 236, 267.
178 Takayasu, 'The Pressures of Change', www.nippon.com/en/features/c00410/.
179 See Iio's discussion in *Nihon no tōchi kōzō*, p. 111 *et passim*.
180 Takayasu, 'The Pressures of Change', www.nippon.com/en/features/c00410/.
181 Estevez-Abe, Hikotani and Nagahisa, 'Japan's New Executive Leadership', p. 254.
182 Takenaka, *Shushō Seiji*, pp. 5, 6.
183 Takenaka argues that 'winning public support became the most important condition [for obtaining and maintaining the post of prime minister]'. *Shushō shihai*, p. 5.
184 Mishima, 'Grading Japanese Prime Minister Koizumi's Revolution', p. 733.
185 Machidori, *Shushō seiji*, p. 99, referring to Takenaka's analysis in *Shushō shihai*, pp. 4–7. See also below.
186 Iio, *Nihon no tōchi kōzō*, p. 201.
187 Krauss and Pekkanen, *The Rise and Fall of Japan's LDP*, p. 239.

3 Reinforcing the power of the prime ministerial executive under the second Abe administration

Abe's first administration

Abe began his first administration of 2006–2007 by showing strong determination to turn the Kantei into a 'White House', telling the Diet in his inaugural speech that 'he intended "to establish political leadership".'[1] His aim was to bolster the prime minister's policymaking authority by deploying the formal power resources generated by administrative reform to his advantage. He appointed five special advisers to the Kantei, four of whom were politicians, three of whom were women and all of whom shared his views. Each was tasked with a specific area of policy: public relations, national security, economic and fiscal policies, abduction issues and educational reform.[2]

However, Abe made the mistake of not deploying these formal power resources in a functional and efficient manner. As Uchiyama reveals, the prime minister 'tried to imitate Koizumi's style of using top-down political methods . . . but he [Abe] was unable to master the skills sufficiently and had no choice but to compromise with *zoku giin* and others'.[3] In fact, the Kantei became dysfunctional during his tenure as prime minister, with a breakdown of the internal structure of administration within the office itself.[4]

Firstly, Abe failed to achieve sufficient communication and coordination amongst the different component parts of the Kantei. His special advisers communicated with him directly without going through the chief cabinet secretary. Likewise, the chief cabinet secretary and deputy chief cabinet secretaries were individually connected to Abe like spokes in a wheel, and so they did not coordinate with each other.[5]

Secondly, Abe thought that he could strengthen the Kantei by practising 'adviser-based politics' (*hosakan seiji*). His objective was to curb the power of the bureaucracy, but as his advisers grew more powerful, discord soon followed. Not only did he appoint a large number of advisers, but he also showed a distinct preference for selecting politicians as advisers, including politicians who belonged to his 'network of friends' – the kind of advisers that he should have avoided at all costs – rather than recruiting able bureaucrats to provide policy expertise.[6] This alienated his own ministers and also the bureaucracy. The ministers thought, 'If the Kantei thinks they can do it alone, they can try. My ministry is the one that actually formulates the bills. No matter how hard the Kantei may try, [their ideas] will never turn into law unless they ask me for help'.[7] In the end, the collapse of the Kantei resulted in the collapse of Abe's administration.[8]

Thirdly, the administration was beset by a series of political setbacks. A 'twisted Diet' with the Upper House in the hands of the opposition allowed Democratic Party of Japan (DPJ) leader Ozawa to make Diet management as difficult as he could. Together with a succession of scandals involving ministers from his 'cabinet of friends', Abe's popularity and that of his administration plunged rapidly to a point of no return.

Abe's second administration

Abe's second administration has benefited from the lessons he learned during his first term in office[9] and has been strongly influenced by his desire to replicate Koizumi's style of Kantei-oriented politics. Takenaka Heizō, for example, writes, 'It is generally thought that "the Abe Cabinet is aiming to realise the same kind of Kantei leadership as the Koizumi government"'.[10] This means adopting a political style where policies are realised on the basis of the Kantei's leadership centring on the prime minister.[11]

Abe also has his own experience of working in the Kantei to call upon, having observed Koizumi's methods closely under his administration, first as deputy chief cabinet secretary and then as chief cabinet secretary.[12] In the Abe Kantei, he is the one with the longest experience of working there. As Tazaki points out,

> He worked as deputy chief cabinet secretary in the Mori and Koizumi cabinets for a total of three years and two months, as chief cabinet secretary in the Koizumi cabinet for 11 months, and as prime minister for one year. While he has had no experience as a minister, in total he had spent more than five years in the Kantei before returning to the seat of prime minister for a second time. In addition to being involved in policymaking as deputy chief cabinet secretary, he also attended summit meetings and encountered the synchronised terrorist attacks on 11 September 2001, which completely changed postwar history. He saw up close in the Kantei the political strife in the LDP that led to Mori Yoshirō's resignation and the work of Koizumi Junichirō who fundamentally changed the way the prime minister operated. His experience in

the Kantei, including the failure he suffered during the first Abe administration, is what makes who Abe is now.[13]

Abe developed the firm belief that '"From now on, we cannot engage in politics unless the Kantei takes the lead, not the party". . . . Kantei leadership in
his first administration was superficial and completely lacked substance. Abe
must have learned from this harsh reality'.[14] Abe's second administration has,
therefore, been a significant advance on his first and even on the Koizumi
administration. He has taken the power of the Kantei a lot further and imposed
much stronger controls over policymaking. As Mikuriya observes, Abe's
'powerful "Kantei leadership" is the most striking characteristic of the second
Abe administration. . . . [T]he Kantei has never been as strong as it is now'.[15]
    Many of the summary descriptions of Abe's administration are the same
as or similar to those used during the Koizumi period. They include 'strong
Kantei' (*tsuyoi kantei*),[16] 'Kantei leadership' (*kantei shudō*), 'Kantei-led politics' (*kantei shudō seiji*), 'the prime minister's Kantei as the single strong
entity (*shushō kantei ikkyō*)'[17] and 'concentration of power in the Kantei'
(*Kantei shūken*).[18] As Curtis argues, 'Political power is concentrated in the
prime minister's office to a degree that has never been true before.'[19] Other
shorthand descriptions focus on the power of the prime minister himself such
as 'prime ministerial leadership' (*shushō shudō*), 'the prime minister as the
single strong entity' (*shushō ikkyō*), 'prime ministerial rule' (*shushō shihai*),
a 'system where Abe is the single strong force' (*Abe ikkyō taisei*)[20] and 'an
administration where Abe is the single strong figure' (*Abe ikkyō seiken*).[21]
Such phrases all refer to a situation where, it is argued, power has become
concentrated in the prime minister.[22] Abe is exerting greater control over the
policymaking process than any of his predecessors.
    In this context, separating the prime minister and the Kantei becomes dif-
ficult. The 'prime minister' and 'prime ministerial executive', which is the
'prime minister plus', merge as one. The Kantei underpins and augments
Abe's power as prime minister, and in a myriad of ways, the prime minister
and his office operate as a 'fused entity'. Indeed, it is the individual and the
collective that make such a formidable team. At the same time, the Kantei
becomes shorthand for the prime minister, his office *and the core government offices* – the Cabinet Secretariat and the Cabinet Office – in other
words, Prime Minister Abe's entire policy support apparatus, which has
become such a powerful and central player in the policy process. In order
to extend his authority in government, Prime Minister Abe has also worked
deliberately to augment the formal power resources available to the prime
ministerial executive, including expanding executive structures to promote
specific policies, as well as mobilising other sources of power, including a
number of informal power resources.[23]

Expanding and empowering the policy infrastructure

As a body under the Kantei's direct control, the Cabinet Secretariat is becoming an increasingly important entity in the Abe administration. Empowered to gather information, undertake policy analysis and provide all kinds of clerical and administrative support to the prime minister and chief cabinet secretary, the secretariat now 'functions as the command centre for realising Abe's signature policies spanning the economy, foreign and security policy.'[24] By 2017 its staff complement had undergone considerable expansion compared with the size of its workforce at the time of the inauguration of the Abe administration in 2012.[25] With a large and dedicated bureaucracy working for the Kantei, the Abe administration has the ability to formulate a response to each and every important issue facing the government.[26]

The Abe administration has also overseen a proliferation of the official duties of ministers of state for special missions and ministers in charge (of certain issues). Almost all Abe ministers carry these other responsibilities. In Abe's cabinet formed on 3 August 2016, for example, only 5 out of 19 were without additional responsibilities in terms of positions as ministers of state and/or ministers in charge (of certain issues).

Another important advance that Abe has made is to expand the number and range of policy councils to provide policy advice, expertise and information outside the usual ministry and agency channels. These councils are an extension of the Kantei and have vastly strengthened its policymaking capabilities. The Abe administration revived the CEFP, after the DPJ attempted to abolish it, positioning it as the headquarters for macroeconomic policy.[27] The government also added another to the category of 'councils on important policies' with the establishment of the Council on National Strategic Special Zones under the National Strategic Special Zones Law, which held its first meeting on 7 January 2014.

In fact, a total of 15 new policy councils (*kaigi*) and headquarters (*honbu*) were launched in the 3 months following the inauguration of Abe's government in December 2012.[28] In addition to the CEFP, they included other important councils supporting Abe's signature policy of 'Abenomics': the Headquarters for Japan's Economic Revitalisation, the Industrial Competitiveness Council and the Regulatory Reform Council (later Regulatory Reform Promotion Council),[29] known as the 'big four'.[30] In many respects, the policy councils that Abe's administration mobilised to promote its signature economic policy were the very basis on which Abenomics was promoted and implemented.[31] Four of the 15 new policy councils, including the Advisory Council on the Establishment of a National Security Council (NSC), were created by prime ministerial decision, with a majority of the remainder set up by a decision of the cabinet. The NSC, which was finally launched in December 2013, substantially enhanced the powers of the prime minister in defence and security matters. The NSC Law (*Kokka Anzen Hoshō Kaigi Setchihō*) promulgated the 'four ministers' meeting involving the prime minister, chief cabinet secretary, Minister of Foreign Affairs and the Minister of Defence for the purpose of 'achieving smooth decision-making under the Kantei's leadership.'[32] It was supported by the establishment of a National Security Secretariat (NSS) in the Cabinet Secretariat in January 2014. Chief Cabinet Secretary Suga Yoshihide described the NSS as firmly supporting his and the prime minister's leadership 'by breaking down the vertically segmented structure of the government offices.'[33] It was charged with the overall coordination and administrative aspects of the NSC's operations and has also served to expand the influence of the Cabinet Secretariat on foreign and security policy.[34] Many Cabinet Secretariat staff are also assigned to the policy councils and headquarters set up by the Abe administration.

By 2016, Abe had on his authority alone, founded a total of 14 councils, while a further 16 were established by the cabinet, 22 were organised on the basis of decisions made by other councils or headquarters, or decisions made by the chief cabinet secretary, or on the basis of a cabinet understanding, while another 15 were set up on an *ad hoc* basis.[35] From a policymaking perspective, these councils buttressed the powers and prerogatives of the prime ministerial executive, particularly the 'big four' councils. The CEFP and the Headquarters for Japan's Economic Revitalisation have been responsible for the Abe administration's 'growth strategy' with specific policy measures discussed in the Regulatory Reform Council[36] and in the Industrial Competitiveness Council established under the Headquarters, which examines proposals for the growth strategy by area.[37] Both of these councils have also been described as 'symbols of the Kantei's leadership'.[38] However, no one council predominates in terms of influence on policy, while the proliferation of council meetings overall is said to be designed to weaken bureaucrats' influence.[39] More generally, what the councils have done is widen the policymaking community, thereby strengthening the intellectual base of national policymaking.[40] The issues examined by the councils run the gamut of national policy and inevitably cut across the policy domains of the established ministries.

The councils also provide a venue for Abe to give instructions to those cabinet ministers who are members to issue general policy directives and to facilitate the taking of executive decisions on policy by Abe and others, including cabinet ministers, *outside a cabinet setting*. This applies particularly to those councils and headquarters that Abe chairs such as the CEFP (which includes five related cabinet members and other cabinet members who can join in as necessary) and the Industrial Competitiveness Council, which Abe chairs together with six related cabinet members including Deputy Prime Minister Asō Tarō.

The Headquarters for Japan's Economic Revitalisation is different from the CEFP, Industrial Competitiveness Council and Regulatory Reform Council in that all of its members are politicians. Prime Minister Abe is the chairman and all cabinet members, including the deputy prime minister, chief cabinet secretary, Minister of State for Economic Revitalisation etc., are members.[41] The Headquarters provides a setting in which the prime minister can give instructions to the relevant cabinet member regarding his/ her response to each policy issue taken up in the Industrial Competitiveness Council. It thus 'guarantees speediness in realising policies and the ability to put policies into practice on the basis of political determination.'[42] Prime Minister Abe has used it, for example, to issue directives to cabinet members to implement measures in areas such as employment support, promotion of active participation by women and other issues.[43] Its secretariat is staffed mainly by officials from the Ministry of Economy, Trade and Industry (METI).[44]

Abe has also followed Koizumi's strategy of setting up councils under the Kantei in order to counter the PARC's policy divisions and weaken the party's policymaking influence.[45] As Uchihashi argues,

> we have seen the rise of the Kantei dictatorship. . . . [with] advisory organs . . . created one after the other in order to provide logistical support for the Kantei's intentions. . . . I have been calling [the reports of these advisory bodies] 'reports made in accordance with [the Kantei's] mood [*sontaku tōshin*]'. . . . The advisory organs are run by people whom the government likes. . . . The reports are 'bureaucrat-made papers' that completely reflect the Kantei's intentions. . . . [T]he government makes policy decisions on the basis of that report, saying that they have sufficiently listened to the people's opinions. It is nothing but ceremony. Cabinet decisions are made for bills on the basis of such reports that are created based on what the Kantei wants, and then they are submitted to the Diet so that they can steamroll the bill. There is no way that the ruling parties, which hold an absolute majority, can oppose the bill. This has become the norm. The government's various advisory bodies are at the forefront of this process.[46]

In a further development along similar lines, Abe has established a policymaking structure within the LDP itself – the group of so-called 'special organs' (*tokubetsu kikan*) – under the direct supervision of the president (*sōsai chokuzoku*).[47] These are 21 mainly 'headquarters' looking at a diverse range of individual policy issues, some of which overlap with those of the Kantei's councils, such as the Administrative Reform Promotion Headquarters and the Headquarters for Japan's Economic Revitalisation. Other headquarters reflect Abe's pet policy projects such as the Headquarters for the Promotion of Revision to the Constitution, the Headquarters for the Revitalisation of Education and the Headquarters for North Korean Abductions. These 'special organs' are designed to ensure that the Kantei's top-down policy direction is transmitted directly into the party. They are evidence that the LDP president (and prime minister) is directly sponsoring and initiating policy deliberations *within the party* and has successfully penetrated the party's internal policymaking apparatus, thus weakening the PARC as a policymaking body and shifting the balance of policymaking power further in favour of the prime minister who now has much greater latitude to pursue his own policy initiatives through an internal party process in addition to executive channels.

Abe's strong personnel support structure

On an interpersonal, informal and unofficial level, an 'inner core elite'[48] in the form of several small groups or 'cliques' who are close to Abe have been highly influential in running his government. The first of these groups was the so-called '3As + 1S' – 'the four politicians who were said to control the Abe administration'.[49] It consisted of Abe himself, Deputy Prime Minister and Minister of Finance Asō and Minister in Charge of Economic Revitalisation and Minister of State for Economic and Fiscal Policy Amari Akira, until his resignation in January 2016. These were the '3As' while Suga was the '1S'. Abe called this group the 'Abe administration's trio'. As he explained,

> Asō acts as the spokesperson for Ministry of Finance but he also knows how to think like a business manager. The ministry approaches [me], but in the end I say, 'Let me decide this with the Minister', then I make the decision with Asō. When someone is as big as Asō, the Ministry of Finance can't overturn his decisions. Amari was one of the people who created the administration as my Election Affairs Headquarters chairman for the leadership election. He is also highly competent in terms of economic policy; Asō can't compete with him when it comes to those kinds of abilities as a technocrat. But the two are completely in the same boat.[50]

When it came to actually running the Abe administration, the trio were regarded as 'in a class of their own', acting in cooperation as the Abe administration's 'mainstay'.[51] Even after Amari resigned, Abe continued to regard him as 'irreplaceable'.[52] Abe mulled over Amari's return in the August 2016 reshuffle, wanting him back in the cabinet, but proceeded with caution because of the likely public backlash.[53] In lieu, Amari was appointed to serve on the LDP's Executive Council where he could facilitate the application of Abe's influence at the highest level of the party's decision-making process and block attempts by Ishiba Shigeru, a potential rival for the LDP presidency, to assume the policy offensive in the council, which Ishiba joined in August 2016.[54] After Amari's resignation, the 3A + 1S became the 2A + 1S and 'are in charge of running the administration.'[55]

Throughout, Suga and Asō have maintained their close partnership supporting the prime minister, and Abe continues to emphasise his bond with Asō, saying things like 'Our relationship is like the Japan-US alliance'.[56] Asō not only advises Abe on fiscal policy but also on the overall management of the administration.[57] After the August 2016 cabinet reshuffle, Suga and Asō continued to form the 'strong team' supporting Abe.

In terms of the day-to-day, inner workings of the Kantei itself, the supreme decision-making body is said to be the 'unofficial meeting with the chief cabinet secretary and deputy chief cabinet secretaries' (*seifuku kanbō chōkan kaigi*)[58] chaired by Abe and held almost every day. The prime minister's Chief Executive Secretary,[59] Imai Takaya,[60] who is a former high-level METI bureaucrat[61] and who previously served as Abe's secretary in his first cabinet on loan from METI,[62] also attends. As Tazaki reveals,

> [T]he majority of important judgements are made during . . . [this] meeting. The meetings are short; they last about 10 to 15 minutes. However, since they are held almost every day, the members can gain a deeper understanding of each other's opinions and also prevent misunderstandings.[63]

The meetings are not publicised but are vitally important because 'when the prime minister, chief cabinet secretary, deputy chief cabinet secretaries and the chief executive secretary to the prime minister come together to discuss matters and decide on policies, their decisions move the entire government.'[64] In other words, this is the most important meeting in the Kantei given its function to determine the administration's basic direction. It is where the prime minister and his closest support staff 'work as one to decide the priority of policies and measures to realise the policies.'[65] The meeting thus 'acts as the headquarters of the Kantei and therefore of the government'.[66] It was during one of these meetings, for example, that the timing of the cabinet decision to change the constitutional interpretation on exercising the right of collective self-defence was decided.[67] Abe has been able to benefit from this informal support structure within the Kantei. Its members are loyal to him and at the same time trust each other and work as one to support him.[68] As Deputy Chief Cabinet Secretary, Hagiuda Kōichi, relates,

> When Abe led his first cabinet, no one gave him candid or stern advice. But under the second Abe cabinet, everyone is very straightforward and

has no hesitation to offer their opinions. We are Abe's old friends but not his 'yes men'. This makes a huge difference.[69]

Agreements reached at the meeting are conveyed in a top-down fashion by the deputy chief cabinet secretary in charge of administration to the assistant chief cabinet secretaries in charge of domestic and international affairs respectively – depending on the policy – whereupon the information is shared with the Office of Assistant Chief Cabinet Secretary.[70] This consists of 30 or so top officials above the level of division chief from various ministries and is headed by the two assistant chief cabinet secretaries.[71]

Another 'trio' – Abe, Suga and Imai – operates as the very 'inner circle' of the Kantei. Whether it is personnel affairs, domestic or foreign policy, decisions on core matters are reportedly made by this group.[72] As Sakano puts it, the Abe administration's policies in practice are decided by the inner circle around the prime minister,[73] with Suga and Imai 'the key persons in the Kantei led by Abe.'[74] If Suga is the public face of the administration then Imai is the 'chief assistant behind the scenes'.[75] He controls information relating to cabinet reshuffles while Suga controls information regarding the appointment of bureaucrats.[76] In reality, Imai's primary task is to handle all manner of political tasks that the administration faces from dealing with the political situation to managing the Diet and the prime minister's schedule, while influencing policies as the prime minister's leading close aide.[77] He has a very good relationship with Abe both publicly and privately, and Abe puts a very high level of trust in him.[78] Imai played a particularly important role in the standoff with the Ministry of Finance (MOF) over raising the consumption tax in 2014. Not only did he usurp a position normally reserved for MOF officials in being appointed as chief executive secretary to the prime minister, but he was also able to pick holes in MOF arguments pushing for the consumption tax rise and thus score victories in arguments with MOF officials. In this way, he contributed significantly to the deteriorating Kantei relationship with the MOF.[79]

In terms of other personnel in the Kantei, Abe has five special advisers. Three are Diet members with expertise in fields such as foreign policy, while two are bureaucrats who specialise in public relations and national infrastructure policies. They were selected based on their skills and are described as 'Abe's five "unsung heroes"'[80] and remained in their positions following the cabinet reshuffle in August 2016.

Abe also expanded the personnel basis of the Kantei by appointing a relatively large number of so-called 'special advisers to the cabinet'.[81] As of October 2013, 11 people had been appointed to this position.[82] Two have acted as Abe's economic counsellors or special advisers on the economy – Hamada Kōichi (professor emeritus at Yale University) who was appointed special adviser to the cabinet and Honda Etsurō (former MOF bureaucrat and university professor) who was formally appointed as adviser to the Cabinet Secretariat.[83] Hamada, Abe's so-called 'mentor' on economic policy, was the 'founder' of Abenomics[84] and its so-called 'theoretical pillar',[85] while Honda, also described as 'Prime Minister Abe's economic policy brains',[86] has been deeply involved in specific policies under the Abenomics umbrella alongside Hamada.[87] To assist in handing foreign and security affairs, Abe appointed Yachi Shōtarō, who had previously been administrative vice-minister of the Ministry of Foreign Affairs (MOFA) during the Koizumi and first Abe cabinets, as a special adviser to the cabinet in December 2012, and later made him secretary-general of the National Security Secretariat, the administrative body supporting the NSC, as well as national security adviser to the cabinet in January 2014. In announcing his appointment, Suga identified Yachi as 'precisely the person who will break down the vertical segmentation of the ministries and agencies'.[88]

Abe in his second administration has shown a distinct preference for able, expertise-based bureaucrats as his advisers rather than politicians. As Mikuriya points out,

Abe succeeded in establishing his own form of Kantei leadership by reviving the Kantei without any politicians who were *seijiya* [a shrewd or manipulative politician who emphasises their own interests]. . . . Abe learned this lesson from his first mistake and established his ideal form of Kantei leadership when he came back for a second attempt.[89]

At the same time, when it comes to his need for expert advice, Abe 'tends not to rely on any particular person, but works by seeking the advice of different experts depending on the issue at hand.'[90]

Supporting the Kantei's initiative in policymaking are powerful advisers such as the Deputy Chief Cabinet Secretary in Charge of Administration, Sugita Kazuhiro, and the Assistant Chief Cabinet Secretaries for Domestic and International Affairs, Furuya Kazuyuki, and Kanehara Nobukatsu, respectively. They liaise not only with bureaucrats but also with influential politicians in the ruling party in order to work out policy details under Chief Cabinet Secretary Suga. The strong relationship between Deputy Chief Cabinet Secretary Sugita[91] and the assistant chief cabinet secretaries is reportedly helping the Kantei take the policy initiative across a range of areas. Another important task for the assistant chief cabinet secretaries is to capture the prime minister's policy intentions and transmit them directly to the Kasumi-gaseki bureaucracy.[92]

As for the top ten visitors to the Prime Minister's Office, data compiled by the *Nihon Keizai Shinbun* over four years from January 2013 until January

2017 show that important figures in Abe's administration also include a former executive secretary in his first administration, Kitamura Shigeru, who is head of the Cabinet Intelligence and Research Office and the most frequent visitor; the current and former administrative vice-ministers of foreign affairs, Sugiyama Shinsuke, and Saiki Akitaka; and Foreign Minister Kishida Fumio. The heavy emphasis on foreign affairs, security and intelligence expertise amongst these visitors underscores Abe's desire to assume direct control over the Foreign Ministry[93] and lead the country's diplomacy personally, which is 'a major departure from the past tradition of letting the foreign and defense ministries take the lead in matters related to diplomacy and security.'[94] Other frequent visitors to the Kantei include Chief Cabinet Secretary Suga, former Deputy Chief Cabinet Secretaries Sekō and Katō, and Asō and Amari.

It is Chief Cabinet Secretary Suga, however, who is the key political operative in the inner circle of Kantei decision-makers and the most important figure in Abe's administration apart from the prime minister himself. Suga is the politician whom Abe trusts the most.[95] His relationship with Abe has been described as lying 'at the heart of the Abe administration'[96] and the secret behind the administration's success in 'realising rule by the Kantei' (*kantei shihai*).[97] The Abe-Suga duo reputedly 'works as one'[98] in managing the Kantei, and the combination works better than any other before it because Suga is completely devoted to Abe who has been heard to praise Suga in terms such as, 'He does everything he can for the Abe government.'[99] LDP Secretary-General, Nikai Toshihiro, has commented, 'The prime minister and the chief cabinet secretary are almost on the same wavelength. That is why the Abe government and the LDP are stable and we feel reassured.'[100]

Abe reputedly accepts Suga's counsel on policy issues and his judgement on political ones. Suga is said to work 'quietly day and night to exercise his influence on powerful individuals and organizations and he shows unfailing loyalty to Abe. This appears to be the greatest source of the Abe administration's stability.'[101] Indeed, Suga's loyalty to Abe is legendary: he backed Abe for the leadership of the LDP in both 2006 and 2012, has declared that he has no intention of becoming prime minister himself and 'is strongly determined to dedicate himself to the role of number two.'[102] He emphasises, 'My mission is to devote myself to Abe'[103] and has been quoted as saying, 'My role is to lay the groundwork for moving the government forward based on the prime minister's policy.'[104] He has also revealed that 'Every day, all I think about is how to support the administration – nothing more, nothing less.'[105] An LDP member close to Suga elaborates, 'He doesn't overstep boundaries; the fact that [Suga] sticks to the stance that he has no intention of becoming prime minister and that he is "only aiming to become the best chief cabinet secretary" now creates a sense of trust.'[106]

Other shorthand descriptions of Suga include 'fixer',[107] 'close adviser', 'chief coordinator'[108] and 'important stabilizing force'.[109] He has employed his considerable personnel management and policy skills in the service of the Abe administration, being largely responsible for delivering 'strong cabinet unity, lack of major policy failures, and overall consistency.'[110] As Mikuriya argues, Kantei leadership in the Abe administration is largely based on Suga's competence. As a result, it is unlike the usual Kantei leadership, prime ministerial leadership and political leadership because 'what Suga is aiming to achieve is control over politics of all kinds – both "everyday politics" and "non-everyday politics".'[111] This makes the Kantei's role completely different from that under Koizumi. For example, the process of drafting laws has completely changed. In the past individual ministries would engage in discussions before the Kantei took over. Nowadays, it is the Kantei that first decides the direction that is to be taken and then hands the matter over to the ministries. If the issue is really important like the TPP then designated teams are set up to work on it. Suga prioritises the speedy handling of issues by a small number of people. In this respect he is exceptional when compared with previous chief cabinet secretaries. As for bureaucrats, he makes them work extremely closely, at times threatening them and reorganising teams for each task.[112] The way in which Suga quickly established control over the Cabinet Secretariat after the Abe administration was inaugurated was important in enabling the Kantei to coordinate and mediate amongst high-ranking bureaucrats.[113]

In dealing with the public, on the other hand, Suga deploys a savvy media strategy. As Mikuriya observes, 'An outstanding aspect of the Abe-Suga regime is their way of dealing with the media'.[114] If an issue arises relating to either domestic or foreign policy – such as the TPP, JA reform, or the North Korean abduction issue – a press conference is organised where Suga comments on the matter. The press conference is designed to give the impression that the government is dealing with the issue and has settled it, whether or not this is actually the case.[115] If there is a scandal or desired policy outcomes have not been achieved, Suga will direct media attention to other policies. For example, a renewed emphasis on Abenomics followed the passage of the new security laws allowing the Japanese Self-Defence Forces to participate in collective self-defence.[116]

While Suga's personal methods, approach and relationship with Abe lie behind his success as chief cabinet secretary, assisting the consolidation of Suga's own power has been the expansion in the importance and authority of his office as a result of the process of administrative reform. As Takayasu writes, 'the expansion of the roles of the core government offices since the 1980s has coincided with the increasingly prominent position of the chief cabinet secretary.[117] The Cabinet Secretariat now provides a large bureaucratic power base for the occupant of this post.

As a body under the Kantei's command, the Cabinet Secretariat also performs a leading operational role in supporting the Kantei's policy initiatives. With its information-gathering, policy analysis, clerical and administrative functions selectively providing policy backup for the prime minister and chief cabinet secretary, the secretariat has assumed the status of a centralised bureaucratic headquarters for assisting the implementation of the key policies of the Abe administration in a range of areas.[118] Its staff members numbered just over 800 when the Abe administration was established, but this figure climbed each year to over 1100 by 2017.[119] Many are assigned to the various policy councils and headquarters set up by the Abe administration[120] to provide policy advice, expertise and information outside the usual ministry and agency channels. With such a large administrative infrastructure focussed on providing policy support for the Kantei, it is equipped to deal with any and all policy issues as they arise.[121]

Suga has also excelled in another area – personnel affairs – and here he has played a pivotal role in consolidating executive power in the Kantei. His particular interest has reportedly been in finding 'a method for controlling bureaucrats and politicians'.[122] He installed and then managed the personnel appointments system for the cabinet, Kantei and the party, acting effectively as 'the headquarters for personnel affairs'.[123] He is particularly skilled in putting 'the right people into the right positions' in order to advance the Abe administration's policy agenda and has built a system for exerting 'control through personnel appointments.'[124] According to one account that quotes a long-serving LDP Diet member,

> Suga's political power is based on his power over personnel appointments and his information-gathering capability. He controls all appointments, from deputy ministers [*fuku daijin*] down, and uses these appointees as sources of information. . . . He [also] decides whether a scandal-tainted cabinet member keeps his job or gets fired. This Diet politician asserts that 'Mr. Suga absolutely outstrips Prime Minister Abe in terms of real political power'.[125]

When asked how he handles personnel affairs Suga answered, 'I make most of the personnel decisions. I have no time to consult the prime minister for every single decision. But I always consult the prime minister beforehand for important personnel decisions for key posts such as Supreme Court Judges. I always tell him about any decisions I make myself, too.'[126] Suga relies ultimately on the prime minister's judgement but also has a reputation for acting decisively to appoint those he prefers and to remove those whose appointments he opposes. In the transition period leading to the establishment of the Abe administration in December 2012 when Japan Post Holdings appointed former MOF bureaucrat, Saka Atsuo, as its president and CEO, Suga complained that the appointment reflected a MOF attempt to reserve the post for retired ministry officials. He then acted quickly to replace Saka with Nishimuro Taizō from the private sector in June 2013.[127] Suga's first act after being appointed as chief cabinet secretary was also to remove Bank of Japan Governor, Shirakawa Masaaki, from his post and to replace him with Kuroda Haruhiko.[128] Suga later broke with tradition by selecting former diplomat Komatsu Ichirō who supported constitutional revision to the position of director-general of the Cabinet Legislation Bureau, instead of the bureau's deputy, in preparation for the reinterpretation of the Constitution to allow the Japanese armed forces to participate in collective self-defence.

It is in relation to personnel appointments in the bureaucracy that Suga's authority has had broad system-wide effects. He has been pivotal in the success of the Abe administration in subordinating the bureaucracy to the Kantei at the same time as mobilising considerable bureaucratic talent to serve its interests. Abe himself, after the experience of his first administration, has also learned how to use bureaucrats without making enemies of them and without being manipulated by them.[129] The upshot is that his administration has achieved what all its predecessors failed to do – subordinate the bureaucracy to the Kantei. When matched against the Abe-Suga combination, the power of the ministries can no longer compete. The message that 'the Kantei will make personnel decisions' was sent around Kasumigaseki less than a month after the Abe administration was inaugurated in December 2012.[130] Suga then deployed the Personnel Affairs Examination Council in the Kantei to reject more appointments proposed by the ministries. This was followed by the establishment of a much more powerful formal body in the Cabinet Bureau of Personnel Affairs in May 2014. The bureau became officially responsible for personnel affairs in ministries and agencies, allowing the Kantei formally to exercise leadership powers in making personnel decisions for the posts of *shingikan* (bureau deputy director-general) and above.[131] In practice its personnel decisions have extended beyond these very senior posts to include 'the leading division directors, who are the ones that actually do the most work in the bureaucratic system.'[132]

The significance of the bureau is that it has further strengthened the Kantei's power,[133] centralised control over executive personnel affairs from a comprehensive perspective and institutionalised a process whereby the Kantei makes all the major personnel decisions for the bureaucracy.[134] Although the bureau has a formal head (Deputy Chief Cabinet Secretary Hagiuda), Suga is the one who virtually heads it.[135] Officially, the process requires the ministries to submit their personnel appointment plans in advance to the prime minister, chief cabinet secretary and relevant ministers to discuss and make the final decision.[136] In practice, Suga, Hagiuda and other officials meet in

Suga's office in the Kantei whenever necessary to decide the appointments of the 670 administrative vice-ministers, bureaux directors-general and deputy directors-general.[137] Their aim is reportedly to select the most capable people to positions where they can deal with the administration's policies in a speedy fashion. However, their real objective is to prioritise the implementation of the Kantei's policies.[138]

Suga revealed that he had established an intelligence network across the various ministries and was constantly gathering information on able bureaucrats so that the most capable bureaucrats are appointed. This was the only way he could make effective use of bureaucrats without significant experience himself as a former bureaucrat and without previously holding many key ministerial posts.[139] He did, however, call on his experience as Minister of Internal Affairs and Communications to follow some broad principles in the art of controlling bureaucrats. As Mikuriya explains, given the propensity of bureaucrats to operate according to their own logic, it is necessary to use personnel decisions as a means of controlling them. This does not require Suga actually to control each and every personnel decision; he merely has to appear to be in control of personnel affairs. So if a ministry sends an incompetent bureaucrat to the Kantei, the Cabinet Bureau of Personnel Affairs undertakes the task of teaching the official a lesson. With the bureau in charge, 'the Kantei has been able to control everything'.[140]

A report in June 2016 revealed just how thoroughly selection processes at the top levels of the bureaucracy had been politicised and how appointments now broke with long-standing conventions of selection. At a news conference on 14 June, Suga repeated that the Kantei was 'now in control of personnel appointments' declaring, 'More strategic appointments are being made to Kasumigaseki as a whole, and this has been established as the norm.'[141] Three in more recent times stand out: the selection of the first woman (a former secretary to the prime minister) to head the Minister's Secretariat at the Ministry of Internal Affairs and Communications (MIAC); the appointment of Abe's former secretary in charge of economic policy at the Kantei as director-general of METI's Economic and Industrial Policy Bureau; and the appointment of Okuhara Masaaki, former director-general of the Management Improvement Bureau of the Ministry of Agriculture, Forestry and Fisheries (MAFF), to the top post of administrative vice-minister. Okuhara had built a reputation as a leading reformer in the ministry.[142] According to a senior MAFF official, his appointment 'was interpreted as "a sign of the Kantei's determination to implement agricultural reforms"'.[143] It stunned the ministry, which had not expected that Okuhara would be promoted to administrative vice-minister from his position as director-general of the Management Improvement Bureau. However, Suga made it clear that this choice was 'the Kantei's decision' given the priority it attached to improving competitiveness in the agricultural sector.[144] Given such appointments, administrative vice-ministers are now regarded as political appointees and are dubbed 'parliamentary vice-ministers of the bureaucracy'.[145] As one METI official quipped, 'If you want to become a vice-minister, you will have to fall into line with the Kantei'.[146]

Inevitably, the changed personnel appointment system and Suga's skills at using personnel affairs as a means of exerting pressure on Kasumigaseki bureaucrats have impacted on how bureaucrats approach their jobs. Suga is now 'feared in Kasumigaseki' because of 'his authority to make personnel decisions.'[147] As Taoka comments,

> bureaucrats now place top priority on saving their necks and being promoted and brown-nose the people in power for that purpose, so they cannot stop [the politicians]. I now understand that perhaps this was the kind of mental state experienced by the pre-war Foreign Ministry bureaucrats who promoted leaving the League of Nations and allying with Germany and Italy and Education Ministry bureaucrats who attacked the 'theory of the Emperor as an organ of government'.[148]

Not surprisingly, there is concern in Kasumigaseki that officials might become timid given that displeasing the Kantei might block their career plans.[149] According to one LDP Diet member, 'after the Kantei seized control over personnel appointments, unpleasant information no longer reaches the Kantei.'[150] A METI official has also revealed that bureaucrats are wary of Suga. Even LDP executives such as former Secretary-General Tanigaki Sadakazu and Chairman of the LDP's Research Commission on the Tax System, Miyazawa Yōichi, learnt how scary it was to take him on. Because of the Cabinet Bureau of Personnel Affairs, the Kantei cannot be challenged.[151] Bureaucrats have become increasingly nervous about the Kantei's opinions of them, increasing the risk of 'excessive deference' to the Kantei.[152]

However, Suga's methods are to encourage bureaucrats as well as to intimidate them. When the LDP returned to government in 2012, he endeavoured to restore the morale of the bureaucracy after their loss of confidence under the DPJ. He told them,

> 'Work in line with the Abe Cabinet's policy'. . . . Those who fell into line saw that personnel affairs were quite well managed. At the same time, they were threatened with the prospect that 'if you don't work properly you will be fired'. As a result, they were inspired to work hard.[153]

On the positive side, bureaucrats can rely on Suga's powers of policy coordination to facilitate the advancement of measures, which, from their viewpoint, 'makes the Abe administration easy to work with.'[154]

Suga has also fashioned the Cabinet Secretariat 'into an instrument of responsive top-down policy leadership',[155] which facilitates both the handling and resolution of policy issues. He handles matters with great speed, to the point where business circles and others take their proposals directly to the Kantei rather than going through METI because they are dealt with quickly and are soon reflected in policy.[156] In fact, many of the Abe government's bold policy changes can be traced back to Suga.[157] The prime minister places full confidence in his chief cabinet secretary on policy matters declaring that 'The Chief Cabinet Secretary and I share exactly the same aspirations'.[158] On those occasions when Abe battles members of his own party whose vested interests will be damaged by reform, Suga frequently takes command from behind the prime minister in the fight against these entrenched interests.[159]

When it came to finding a way to realise JA reform in 2014–2015, for example, it was Suga who instructed the MAFF to work as one in order to get through the difficult politics associated with this policy issue.[160] He summoned Okuhara to the Kantei almost every day and gave instructions regarding the direction of the reform.[161] In response to Abe's policy wishes, Suga also assumed command from behind the prime minister in the fight against the Central Union of Agricultural Cooperatives (JA Zenchū),[162] not conceding on the issue of abolishing it, which the prime minister was determined to realise.[163] Moreover, when Abe gave instructions to MAFF Minister Hayashi Yoshimasa in May 2014 to implement regulatory reforms in agriculture, he added that he wanted the minister to 'coordinate with Chief Cabinet Secretary Suga and work on putting these reforms into practice'.[164] At the time, rumours were circulating that the Kantei did not consider Hayashi to be very reliable, so the prime minister probably judged that Hayashi could not fight with MAFF bureaucrats and the LDP's 'agricultural tribe' (*nōrin zoku*) on his own.[165] In fact Suga was reputedly even 'more enthusiastic about JA reform than Abe'.[166] As the son of a strawberry farmer, he was passionate about turning agriculture into a growth industry and was, therefore, strongly motivated to reform the agricultural cooperative organisation. This reportedly 'led him to exercise leadership behind the scenes.'[167] Suga referred in press conferences to the need for fundamental reform of the agricultural cooperatives for the benefit of farmers, local co-ops and the 'development of Japan's agricultural industry'.[168] He also had a good relationship with Nikai, chairman of the LDP's Executive Council at the time, who is a political heavyweight known for his coordination skills and someone who would 'never betray' Abe.[169] The administration's JA reform law passed smoothly through the council because of backstage dealing between Suga and Nikai.[170] Suga himself later explained the assistance he received from Nikai revealing,

On the issue of agricultural reform, opinion varies within the party. I've been keeping this a secret, but I sought advice from Nikai when he was leading the party's Executive Council, and he helped me coordinate opinions. On the issue of reduced tax rates, though this is not known to the public, I also sought his advice.[171]

These comments reveal Suga's skills at policy coordination with a key power broker in the party, which eased the path for other Abe administration policies as well, such as Japan-China relations.[172]

Equally important have been Suga's strong connections with the Kōmeitō and its support group Sōka Gakkai, which have facilitated policy agreements between the coalition party and the government. Suga is on excellent terms with Sōka Gakkai Vice-Chairman Satō Hiroshi, a relationship that is 'the key to LDP-Komeito cooperation in elections'[173] and to the passage of certain legislation such as the so-called 'casino bill' in December 2016, even though it was opposed by Kōmeitō leader Yamaguchi Natsuo. The Suga-Kōmeitō connection was also one of the keys to resolving the issue of what tax exemptions would be adopted when the consumption tax prospectively rose to 10 per cent in April 2017. Suga, having backed the Kōmeitō's position, which called for exemptions on fresh and processed foods except alcohol and restaurant meals, imposed his view on the MOF, while Abe ordered former LDP Secretary-General Tanigaki also to accept the Kōmeitō's position. As Toshikawa reports, acting as 'Abe's enforcer', Suga was reportedly 'determined to plunge forward and accept the Komeito's position, even if that move rankled fiscal hawks inside the LDP.'[174] After summoning the MOF administrative vice-minister and Tax Bureau director-general to his office and giving them orders in a raised voice asserting that it was a matter requiring a political decision, Suga threw them out of his office when they objected to the Abe-Suga-Kōmeitō position.[175]

This battle between the MOF and Suga over the consumption tax was more than symbolic of the MOF's defeat and its subordination to the Kantei.[176] It reflected the fact that the MOF's wishes could no longer necessarily prevail on tax policy issues and was the most significant victory that the Abe-Suga duo had scored against the bureaucracy given that the MOF was 'the strongest government office' and the 'government office amongst government offices'.[177] It had reigned over other ministries because of its budget-making authority and had also exercised strong influence over politicians for that reason.

Nor was it the Kantei's only victory against the MOF. In the autumn of 2013, the ministry was forced to yield to Abe and Suga who had adopted a hard-line stance on abolishing the special corporate tax for reconstruction a year early. At the time, this was the ministry's second defeat following the appointment of the Bank of Japan Governor Kuroda.[178] It was also a similar story on the issue of granting a ¥30,000 social welfare benefit to elderly people on small pensions, which was announced in late 2015, where, once again, the Abe-Suga duo prevailed. At the time, the Japanese press reported,

> The Kantei is the one with the political power to determine the priority of items in the budget. The opinion that 'it is hard to take a hack at areas where the Kantei has a strong view' can be heard from within MOF.[179]

The same report revealed a comment from a former Japanese prime minister that 'If the Kantei had this much power when I was prime minister, I could have done more for fiscal reconstruction'.[180] The MOF lost another battle over raising the consumption tax in late May 2016 just prior to the July Upper House election. After this succession of important policy defeats, the ministry's diminished influence over the Kantei reputedly caused despair amongst its officials.[181]

The MAFF has suffered similar policy humiliation at the hands of the Kantei, which pushed ahead with the plan to allow corporations to acquire farmland without first consulting with the MAFF, which caused considerable exasperation in the ministry. The revised Agricultural Land Law (*Nōchihō*) raised the permitted ownership stake of private companies in agricultural production corporations to less than 50 per cent from less than 25 per cent as of 1 April 2016. The easing of regulations was designed to facilitate the entry of companies into the farm sector. From the MAFF's perspective, it amounted to an 'aggressive' easing of regulations, which, in its opinion, would 'confuse farming communities and undermine trust between companies and farmers'.[182] Even MAFF Minister Moriyama Hiroshi was opposed to the farmland ownership program.

The electoral support factor

Given that electoral strength and a strong public support base have grown more important in determining the power of the party leader and prime minister as a result of electoral reform, Abe's authority and standing in the LDP have been considerably boosted by successive victories in general elections, which have given him a strong foundation within the ruling party. In the first instance, the 2009 victory was pivotal. Releasing the LDP from the fetters of its ignominious defeat in 2009 has been an important reason why LDP members are reluctant to oppose Abe. As Mikuriya argues, because 'the party returned to power thanks to Abe. . . . This has had the effect of making the party psychologically indebted to Abe'.[183] LDP politicians felt demoralised and marginalised in opposition, suffering a big drop in the number of visits from bureaucrats and petitioners seeking favours as well as invitations to appear on TV.[184]

The spectre of the squabbling and dysfunctional DPJ also drove home to LDP Diet members the fact that 'division is death' because it alienates voters and leads to electoral defeat. Hence the need to exercise self-control and avoid intense conflict within the party as much as possible if LDP Diet members wanted to remain in power.[185] The LDP's own record of electoral division over the issue of postal privatisation during the Koizumi adminis- tration and the fear of loss of endorsement and promotion also weighed on the minds of Diet members. As Tazaki observes,

> LDP members are obedient to the Kantei led by Abe. The trauma caused by the postal privatisation, where members who disobeyed the prime minister at the time lost, the concern that deepening the confrontation within the party may lead to losing the people's confidence and hence losing the seat of power, and the fear that they may be treated coldly when personnel decisions are made lie at the bottom of the Diet mem- bers' hearts.[186]

Such an account helps to explain the very low levels of internal debate within the LDP on policies and why 'Abe is the single strong force in the party [*Abe ikkyō taisei*].'[187] As former LDP Secretary-General Koga Makoto observes, 'There is barely any internal debate in today's LDP. At this rate we will fall into despotism'.[188] According to former Prime Minister Koizumi,

> Members of the LDP used to be free to say whatever they wanted to the prime minister. . . . Now, it is weird how they make no noise about what the prime minister wants from the beginning or even before things are finalised.[189]

Overriding all other factors, however, is the LDP's fear of, once again, becoming an opposition party.[190] Since returning to power, LDP politicians have become strongly averse to ever becoming an opposition party again and so a spirit of everyone getting along has become firmly ingrained in the party.[191] They are afraid of a party split and the inevitable loss of power, hence they tend to form a loose consensus on all issues 'from Abenomics to Abe-politics [*Abe no poritikusu*]'.[192] That's the reason 'why they have to come together as a "strong" LDP led by Abe [*"tsuyoi" Abe Jimintō*]'.[193]

Senior Diet members in the party harbour these fears as much as the rank and file politicians, particularly those whom Abe has appointed to important posts such as such as Asō as Minister of Finance and Hosoda Hiroyuki, who was LDP secretary-general during the days of the Asō Cabinet, as executive acting secretary-general (temporarily replacing Secretary-General Tanigaki in July-August 2016) and then as chairman of the LDP's Executive Council.

For these senior members of the LDP, 'Abe is a lifesaver'.[194] They feel a tremendous debt of gratitude to him for making them part of the ruling party again and for this reason could never act against him in order to bring him down.[195] Hosoda, for example, supported the initiation of a discussion in the LDP on the issue of removing the term limit on the party presidency, which was traditionally restricted to two terms or six years,[196] because of his gratitude for being able to make a political comeback. He claims to have 'learned his lesson' and warned against dragging Abe down because of the risk of becoming an opposition party again.[197] This seemed to be the general attitude in the party as well. As a result,

> If Abe says 'right' everyone else says, 'Well, I guess that's okay', and turns right. The reason for this mindset is clear; at this point in time, 'maintaining the Abe administration' has become the most important goal. This idea runs through the LDP as the most important behavioural principle. . . . rebelling against the prime minister's policies would throw the party into confusion. . . . [E]ven if one person objects to the prime minister, the party will certainly and immediately be embroiled in strife. . . . [I]f the LDP administration is focused on maintaining the administration, they do not want any confusion or objections for now. The Abe administration is completely preoccupied with maintaining itself in power. . . . It does not allow people to raise objections, does not make enemies, and does not touch on successors.[198]

Since 2012, the record of the LDP's electoral performance under Abe's leadership has underscored this trend, setting new benchmarks for ruling party popularity and reinforcing the need for compliance with the Abe-led executive. The LDP's landslide victory in the December 2012 Lower House election was followed by further electoral gains: in the July 2013 Upper House election, in the December Lower House 2014 election and in the Upper House election of 2016 when the LDP consolidated its power by gaining a single-party majority for the first time in 27 years and the ruling coalition almost a two-thirds majority to match its two-thirds majority in the Lower House.

Moreover, as long as it is widely believed in the LDP that the Abe administration will continue to be in power tomorrow, ruling party Diet members cannot turn their backs on Abe and the Kantei leadership structure.[199] The loyalty of cabinet ministers, bureaucrats and ruling party politicians is strongly influenced by their expectations that the prime minister will remain in office for a certain period of time. This is because their career prospects are crucially dependent on the stability and longevity of the prime minister's position.[200]

Delivering victories in successive elections has thus provided a strong and stable political base for the Abe administration, putting the prime minister in a predominant position in his own party and paving the way for effective policy leadership by the prime ministerial executive. Election victories have enabled Abe and his close associates to conclude that the Kantei's leadership control over the ruling parties, the Diet and Kasumigaseki is guaranteed.

The power balance between the party and the Kantei is now summed up as 'government high and party low' (*seikō tōtei*) or 'strong government and weak party'.[201] This means that 'the LDP has been significantly weakened while the Kantei has gained an overwhelming level of power.'[202] In early 2015 after the LDP's Lower House electoral victory in December 2014, Abe reportedly 'said with a smug look that he had "gained the people's confidence". . . . Those close to him excitedly thought, "Now the Kantei's leadership that will enable it to control the ruling parties, Diet and Kasumigaseki is guaranteed".'[203]

The continuing popularity of the Abe cabinet in the public opinion polls has only served to reinforce this trend, enabling the Abe executive to dominate the LDP completely. As a result, the party is reportedly overwhelmed by the Kantei's power.[204] Abe has become virtually unchallengeable as government leader, which empowers him to advance his policy agenda, particularly his keystone policies.[205] Sustained public support for his signature platform of 'Abenomics' has strengthened his hand as a reformer and assisted him in confronting vested interests including many interest groups hostile to reform and their political allies in the LDP.

Garnering public support thus assists Japanese prime ministers in leading their own parties and in pursuing their policy goals, with a robust electoral mandate allowing them greater space to demonstrate their policy leadership and deliver on their policy programs.[206] A popular support base can even substitute for a strong party or factional support base, as it did with Nakasone and even Koizumi.[207] Public popularity, electoral successes, strength of a political base and a high public profile are all informal power resources that can be mobilised to underpin prime ministerial leadership.[208] If prime ministers can tap into these informal power resources at the same time as marshalling institutional power resources, their leadership becomes almost unassailable in their own parties.[209]

One of Koizumi's biggest power resources, for example, was his high level of public support, which enabled him to promote policies that met strong resistance from within his party. Furthermore, Koizumi 'made optimal use of the populist technique of directly appealing to the people for support.'[210] Abe is different: he does not deploy public support as a political weapon against his own party but uses it positively in order to engender support amongst

LDP Diet members for the Kantei's reform program, thus making the job easier by reducing intra-party resistance to his policy proposals. Abe also prefers to take his own party with him through persuasion rather than calling those who might disagree with him 'forces of resistance' (*teikō seiryoku*) and enlisting public support in opposition to these elements. While the Koizumi administration resolutely pursued top-down decision-making regardless of opposition from within the LDP, ramming through postal reforms, Abe does not force through reforms in this way. LDP Vice-President Kōmura Masahiko compared Abe with Koizumi as a leader saying,

> Prime Minister Abe is in fact similar to former Prime Minister Koizumi in that both seek reforms and face strong resistance. One difference between them is while Mr. Koizumi labelled opponents within the LDP 'forces of resistance', Mr. Abe tries to talk directly with opposing members or to seek understanding from the LDP leadership, thereby trying to minimize 'resistance'. A good example is agricultural cooperative reform, which has passed the critical point as Mr. Abe has convinced the Central Union of Agricultural Cooperatives [JA Zenchū] and LDP lawmakers affiliated with farm organizations [to accept reforms].[211]

Furthermore, as Miura elaborates,

> If JA reform had been advanced under the Koizumi administration, the prime minister would have proudly declared that he would not compromise with resistance forces and then carried out policymaking in a theatrical manner where he waged a battle against the villain, influential *zoku giin* siding with the resistance force. However, compared to the Koizumi administration the Abe administration has a strong foundation within the ruling party. Furthermore, following the previous Lower House election, the Kantei has become the single strong body in an environment where the LDP is the only strong party. The LDP no longer has interesting villains or members that can be called the 'Don [= boss] of something'. Even opposing opinions only go as far as calling for a cautious response.[212]

In the wake of the LDP's performance in the 2016 Upper House election, the possibility was raised of revising the LDP's bylaws to allow its president to stand for a third term, or nine years in total, or, alternatively, to abolish all restrictions on the president's term of office. These options were openly canvassed by key figures in the LDP including Kōmura, Hosoda and Nikai who successfully engineered a consensus in the ruling party in favour of extending the president's term. As a first step, a meeting of LDP Diet members in October 2016 agreed to extend the maximum term of office to three consecutive terms, or nine years. Kōmura told the meeting, 'realising bold reform requires strong leadership and a certain period of time'.[213] The LDP's annual convention in March 2017 subsequently approved the change with a handclap from the 3500 LDP Diet members and representatives of the party's local branches attending. Nikai declared, '*Abe sōri no ato wa Abe sōri*' ['Prime Minister Abe will be followed by Prime Minister Abe'].[214] The rule change will potentially enable Abe to remain in office until September 2021, becoming Japan's longest-serving prime minister providing he is re-elected president in September 2018 and wishes to run for a third term.

Nikai who backed the option of abolishing all limits on the president's tenure not only wields virtually unmatched influence in the party as one of its senior executives (as Executive Council chairman and then as secretary-general from August 2016)[215] but also maintains good connections with the opposition parties, which will be vital to the success or failure of Abe's bid for constitutional reform.[216] Given Nikai's unswerving loyalty to Abe, his appointment as Abe's 'lieutenant' in the party, particularly in relation to Diet management and election strategy, both areas in which Nikai excels, is regarded as having led to a further concentration of power within the LDP leadership structure by weakening the power of other senior officials and potential rivals and subordinating the party even more to the Kantei.[217]

Besides the JA reform issue, in which he played a supportive role, Nikai has served the Kantei loyally with respect to several other key policy issues. He took the initiative to facilitate Abe's policies in relation to the new security laws and backed the postponement of consumption tax increases[218] together with the administration's 'positive fiscal (i.e. expansionary public spending) policies', thus helping to consolidate the Kantei's control over budget compilation.[219] When the LDP's executive appointments were announced in August 2016, Abe, while resisting the demands of the Kishida faction to appoint their leader as LDP secretary-general, described Nikai as 'the person with the best political skills in the LDP'.[220] Abe expected him to play an important role in smoothing opposition within the party to the Kantei's policy initiatives at the same time as blocking generational change in the LDP by denying Kishida the secretary-general's position.[221] As it happens, Abe's continuing strong grip on the levers of power is undermining potential challengers to his office, including Kishida and Ishiba.

The weakening of factional power centres

The role of LDP factions as internal power structures within the party, which have traditionally generated a strong counterweight to prime ministerial power and undermined ministers' loyalty to the prime minister, has been greatly challenged during Abe's term of office. Unlike the customary tenures of LDP prime ministers, there is no strong anti-mainstream faction to counter Abe's authority and undermine his position. The factions have been successfully subdued as a potential counterweight to Abe's leadership of both the party and the government. One LDP faction member lamented, 'Usually the factions would speak up more and there would be a balanced internal party debate' [but] . . . [t]he current situation can be described as "Abe the all-powerful"'.[222] No one is prepared to stand up to the prime minister 'because the repercussions are too great'.[223]

Abe has been able to subdue the factions in several ways. First he has asserted the revamped powers of the LDP president. The party leadership – Abe as president together with the secretary-general – decides the electoral endorsements of LDP candidates, while Abe as LDP leader and prime minister exercises sole authority over personnel decisions relating to the party executive and ministers in his government respectively.[224] As a result, the LDP has reached the stage where factions can no longer guarantee a politician's future, which has impacted directly on the role and influence of faction leaders, since securing cabinet and other positions for their members has traditionally been a hallmark of their power. As Mikuriya points out,

> The factions that used to be the source of prime ministerial candidates now exist in name only. . . . Today, the role of faction leaders has become akin to that of a landlord [who only provides members with a place to stay instead of guaranteeing faction members' future]. They are surprisingly apathetic. . . . Politicians cannot depend on this kind of person for the future, so they have to stay in their ministerial posts for as long as possible. . . . Therefore, ministers who are part of the Abe administration need to work as hard as possible in the posts that they currently hold. . . . This is because they have no guarantee for the future.[225]

Given these trends, ministers now see themselves as working much more for the prime minister and for his administration.[226] Likewise, because ministerial appointments now depend on criteria largely unrelated to factions, those who are appointed have greater loyalty to the prime minister. This is a development that portends the collapse of the LDP's traditional career path. As Tazaki explains,

> Even factional leaders with power will not have an opportunity to exercise their power unless they are appointed to a post. That is why LDP members cannot openly revolt against Abe unless they have given up on being appointed to a post.[227]

Secondly, Abe has been able to capitalise on precedents set by Koizumi in disregarding factional considerations and factional nominations when it

comes to cabinet and other senior appointments. During the Koizumi administration, the prime minister's personnel decisions were significant because
they demonstrated that 'the authority of the prime minister/LDP leader to
make personnel decisions in the party and the cabinet has become firmly
established',[228] and non-factional considerations were more important as the
basis of his personnel decisions. While faction leaders still lobby Abe for
posts for their members and he is not indifferent to considerations of factional
balance in his personnel choices,[229] like Koizumi, Abe does not pay heed to
the recommendations of factions and their leaders when it comes to choosing
ministers and party executives. He is largely guided by non-factional principles such as selecting people with a similar ideological worldview,[230] offering positions to sworn allies and close associates, harnessing individual Diet
members' strengths and abilities, punishing or promoting LDP politicians
for their electoral performance, reducing opportunities for potential rivals to
challenge his position as LDP president, meddling in factions' internal affairs
by elevating some and not others,[231] rewarding those who have strongly supported his return to office and retention of the prime ministership (such as
Suga, Asō, Amari and Nikai) and paying heed to affirmative action principles
in appointing women to key posts.[232]

Thirdly, Abe's own factional connections are relatively weak. In recent
times he has nominally belonged to the Mori-Machimura-Hosoda faction
(now Hosoda faction)[233] – the Seiwa Seisaku Kenkyūkai, or Seiwakai – but
factional links have rarely advantaged him in his political career[234] and so
he has no great factional loyalties. Abe also suspended his membership of
the Seiwakai on becoming prime minister[235] and was able to reshuffle his
cabinet in September 2014 with a relatively high degree of freedom because
he was not part of a faction.[236] Both Suga and Amari, members of the 3A
+ 1S and core individuals in the Kantei until Amari's resignation, also left
their factions.[237]

Fourthly, Abe has dealt with the factions and their residual powers
quite adeptly by making adroit appointments from amongst the factions. For
example, the most likely intra-party group to perform the role of an anti-
mainstream faction – the Kishida faction (Kōchikai), traditionally a group
of dovish politicians that takes a moderate diplomatic line and which is led
by Foreign Minister Kishida – 'has been given exceptionally favourable
treatment in the awarding of ministerial posts'.[238] Normally such a faction
would have been strongly opposed to a prime minister who takes a much
harder line on foreign and defence policy issues, particularly as Kishida is
a post-Abe contender and has indicated his desire to be the prime minister.[239] However, when a faction receives such favourable treatment then 'no
one is going to defy the administration'.[240] Not surprisingly, the Kishida
faction, which would have been expected to lead the charge against Abe

from within the party, has been accommodating him.[241] It has been deprived of the motivation and momentum to mobilise against Abe because of his biased appointments in its favour, thus 'preventing the formation of opposition elements.'[242]

Finally, Abe has been able to take advantage of the fact that the LDP has now gone through a generational transition, with 'no one left in the party who is overwhelmingly powerful'.[243] Those who could have generated countervailing power to Abe, such as former Prime Minister Mori, former Secretary-General Koga, former chairman of the general assembly of Upper House members, Aoki Mikio, former Secretary-General Katō Kōichi and former deputy LDP leader Yamazaki Taku have all left politics.[244]

Political appointments to buttress the power of the Abe Kantei

Abe is also known for 'personnel decisions by the Abe Kantei' (*Abe Kantei jinji*)'.[245] This is a general description for Abe's skill in making astute political appointments and removals for the purpose of buttressing his position as LDP president and the Kantei's power against possible rivals and rival power centres, and over policies.

One of Abe's most important selection principles has been to tap into the accumulated experience of senior party figures. He set up a so-called 'senior circle' (*shinia sākuru*)[246] made up of those who had been prominent in previous LDP administrations or in the party. In December 2012, he appointed and has continued to reappoint former Prime Minister Asō as deputy prime minister and Minister of Finance as well as utilising the skills of former Prime Minister Fukuda Yasuo in supporting his diplomacy with China and with the United States.[247] Abe also chose former LDP leader Tanigaki as Minister of Justice and then as LDP secretary-general, enabling the prime minister to predominate in the management of his administration by keeping the LDP under his control, something that was made possible by 'Tanigaki's accepting the Kantei's wishes all the time'.[248]

The system has also worked on the members of the senior circle taking turns in major posts in the cabinet and in the party without consideration for factional ties.[249] In September 2014, for example, Nikai 'joined the senior circle when he made a comeback as chairman of the LDP's Executive Council'.[250] His position in the circle was further entrenched by his appointment as LDP secretary-general in August 2016, replacing Tanigaki. At the same time, Abe's canny personnel selections ensured that the Kantei-centred political regime would be maintained. Other leadership positions in the party were distributed evenly amongst the heavyweights in other factions instead of appointing Diet members close to Nikai, where they could potentially form an intra-party counterweight to the Kantei.[251]

Besides setting up the 'senior circle', another of Abe's selection principles has been to adopt a two-tiered system of ministerial appointments, or 'senior ministers system' (*shinia minisutā sei*).[252] His selection of Minister in Charge of Economic Revitalisation Amari and LDP Vice-President in Charge of Diplomacy Kōmura was based on the trust Abe placed in them and their careers up to that point. As a result, they were able to exercise power as the 'seniors' of the METI and MOFA ministers respectively, acting in these roles on various issues including the TPP negotiations and granting Japan the right of collective self-defence respectively.[253]

Abe has also sought to win over major potential rivals by offering them high-level positions. Tanigaki's appointment as LDP secretary-general in the reshuffle of the party's executive line-up in September 2014 was explained by this principle as was Abe's choice of Ishiba Shigeru as Minister in Charge of Regional Revitalisation in the cabinet reshuffle in that month. As both politicians had the potential to become rivals in the LDP presidential election in September 2015, these personnel decisions were truly skilful in terms of ensuring Abe's victory in that election.[254] Abe successfully won over both his major rivals in this way, demonstrating his adroitness in making appointments designed to maintain his predominance in politics against possible future challengers.[255]

On the other hand, in a manner reminiscent of Abe's first administration in 2006–2007, he continues to practise 'friendship-based personnel affairs' (*otomodachi jinji*), but this time to his advantage. Amongst examples of such appointments is Abe's selection of Yamamoto Yūji, an 'amateur in agricultural policy'[256] from the Ishiba faction, as Minister of Agriculture, Forestry and Fisheries in his third cabinet in August 2016. Prior to the LDP leadership election in September 2006 (to replace Koizumi), Yamamoto had set up a 'Parliamentary Group That Supports Challenge Again' (Saicharenji Shien Giren), which was informally known as an 'Abe cheer squad' and which was influential in Abe's selection as LDP president. Yamamoto and Abe continued to be close, meditating together at a Zen temple in Tokyo, and both share similar ideas.[257] In addition, Yamamoto's appointment served the dual purpose of undermining Ishiba's faction, given that Ishiba is Abe's most serious rival for the presidency.[258]

Abe also makes politically strategic appointments in a way cleverly designed to achieve his policy objectives or to remove obstacles in their way. Kuroda's appointment as Bank of Japan Governor can partly be explained by Abe's desire to implement 'bold monetary easing' as the first arrow of Abenomics, an option strongly advocated by Kuroda. In addition, because diplomacy and security are other policy issues where Abe has clear preferences, he wants compliant ministers who will fall into line with his wishes in these areas as well. His aim is to implement 'Kantei-led diplomacy'

(*Kantei gaikō*) led by himself and Suga, thus centralising diplomacy and security under Kantei leadership.[259] In October 2015, Abe also removed Noda Takeshi, chairman of the LDP's Research Commission on the Tax System, because he had refused to follow Abe's instructions on exemptions to an increased consumption tax. In this way, Abe began dismantling the commission known as 'the largest sanctuary within the party'.[260] This followed earlier action against the commission on the corporate tax issue.[261]

In the difficult areas of agricultural policy and agricultural trade reform, Abe approached Nishikawa Kōya to become MAFF Minister in the cabinet reshuffle of September 2014, leading him to completely change sides from being a flag-bearer of LDP opposition to the TPP, as a leading *nōrin zoku* and chairman of the party's TPP Affairs Committee, to promoting it.[262] His appointment was described as symptomatic of the 'Kantei's skilful personnel strategy of giving government posts to "faultfinders" critical of the administration and winning them over to the administration's side in order to silence their criticism.'[263] Besides Nishikawa, other TPP critics were given the posts of MAFF senior vice-minister and parliamentary secretary respectively. In other words, the Abe administration cleverly stopped the criticism from these politicians 'by "promoting" them.'[264]

In his 'tell-all' manuscript on the TPP negotiations, Nishikawa who served Abe well at the core of the TPP negotiations and who was also appointed chairman of the Lower House Special Committee on the TPP (TPP Tokubetsu Iinkai) revealed that he was asked by Abe to 'put together (*shūyaku*) opinions in the party on the TPP'.[265] As he explained, 'The reason the prime minister asked [me] to consolidate opinions was to "fight *zoku giin* members with *zoku giin* members"'.[266] In his request to Nishikawa, Abe used phraseology based on the saying '*doku o motte doku o seisu*' meaning 'fight fire with fire', except that the prime minister used the phrase '*zoku o motte zoku o seisu*',[267] which meant that he wanted to use a prominent *nōrin zoku kanbu* (agricultural policy tribe executive) who was aligned with him to bring the other *nōrin zoku* under the Kantei's control. As Abe reasoned, '*Zoku giin* members can only be restrained by *zoku giin* members'.[268]

Abe also instructed Nishikawa to play the central role in making preparations for submitting the bills relating to JA reform to the ordinary Diet session scheduled to begin on 26 January 2015.[269] This was another reason behind Abe's selection of Nishikawa as minister – to put him in charge of JA reform, which the Kantei was promoting. Nishikawa, who had 'converted' to a pro-reform stance,[270] put his foot down on the accelerator as soon as he was appointed, with Abe, who wanted JA reform to be one of his administration's main achievements, backing up Nishikawa's efforts.[271] The new minister was fully persuaded into this course of action by the Kantei's 'strong determination' on the issue, deciding 'to carry out the reform resolutely and to express his strong will to do so.'[272] Other *nōrin zoku* members objected to Nishikawa's statements on how JA reform should be implemented saying, 'It's not right to allow him to say such things before presenting it to the party'.[273]

Once more taking on the agricultural cooperatives and their allied farm politicians, as well as containing 'faultfinders' during discussions on TPP countermeasures,[274] Abe appointed non-farm politician and up-and-coming LDP star, former Prime Minister Koizumi's son and representative of a metropolitan seat in Yokohama, Koizumi Shinjirō, as head of the party's Agriculture and Forestry Division. Koizumi quickly became infamous for asserting that the Central Bank for Agriculture and Forestry (Nōrinchūkin Bank) was useless while calling for 'robust agricultural reforms', putting him on the same page as the prime minister and chief cabinet secretary. Abe also enlisted Director-General of the MAFF's Management Improvement Bureau Okuhara as his adviser. This was similarly reflective of Abe's desire to co-opt like-minded personnel in his quest for agricultural reform, given that Okuhara was strongly supportive of Abe's reforms to JA and had played an active role in bringing the MAFF into line on the Kantei's proposed reforms to JA in 2014–2015. The appointments of both Koizumi and Okuhara exposed the Kantei's plan to form 'a team . . . to counteract Diet members lobbying for agricultural interests.'[275] Suga, who had promoted Okuhara to the MAFF administrative vice-minister's position, instructed him to support Koizumi and reportedly said, 'I told [Koizumi] to do [the reform] boldly . . . I'm the eldest son of a farmer. I won't let anyone say we can't carry out reform'.[276] Nor did Abe hesitate to appoint another *nōrin zoku* executive as MAFF Minister – Moriyama Hiroshi – who had served, for example, as chairman of the LDP's JA Reform etc. Bill Examination Project Team.

At other times, Abe has selected 'Abe girls' and 'favourites' to key positions in order to promote particular policies and policy reforms as well as to undermine anti-reform elements in the LDP. For example, he appointed Takaichi Sanae, who is close to the prime minister given their shared position on historical revisionism, as PARC chairwoman in December 2012 immediately after the LDP came to power, a position in which she remained until September 2014. During her tenure, the feeling amongst some LDP Diet members was that the party's involvement in the policymaking process continued to decline as a number of important policy matters were being handled in an exceptional manner by Takaichi.[277] Takaichi was later appointed as Minister of Internal Affairs and Communications, distinguishing herself by threatening TV companies with revocation of their broadcasting licenses if they engaged in biased reporting, implying that critical or negative coverage of the Abe administration would qualify as political 'bias'.[278]

Similarly, Abe appointed Inada Tomomi, another female politician who shares his ideological worldview, as Minister in Charge of Regulatory

Reform (and simultaneously chairwoman of the Regulatory Reform Council) in his first cabinet 'so that the council would become practically one with the Kantei'.[279] Later, in the September 2014 reshuffle of LDP executives, he replaced Takaichi with Inada as PARC chairwoman in order to ensure a smooth path for JA reform. Inada was later chosen by Abe to serve as Minister of Defence where she would unquestioningly support Abe's policy initiatives and where he could groom her for even higher office in the party and in the government, including the prime ministership.

In September 2014, Abe also moved MAFF Minister Hayashi back into the party as chairman of the LDP's Research Commission on Agriculture, Forestry and Fisheries Strategy, which was responsible for party agricultural, forestry and fisheries policies. Former METI bureaucrat Saitō Ken continued to occupy the post of chairman of the Agriculture and Forestry Division until appointed as senior vice-minister of the MAFF in the August 2016 cabinet reshuffle. Abe's selection of Saitō to both these positions was an attempt to pursue the cause of agricultural reform with the help of industry circles[280] and was further evidence of Abe's strategy of appointing non-agriculture-linked, pro-reform politicians to key positions in the field of agricultural policy, which had previously been exclusively dominated by *nōrin zoku*. The fact that Hayashi and Saitō, who were not *nōrin zoku* and did not rely on the agricultural cooperatives to back them in elections, occupied key agricultural policy posts, both in the party and in the government, suggested that these personnel decisions were made in order to signify the Kantei's clear intention to continue JA reform.[281]

Individual themes that are emblematic of the Abe administration's policy initiatives and PR campaigns are also supported by the creation of new ministerial duties relating to specific policies. In his various cabinet reshuffles Abe has established new posts such as Minister in Charge of Overcoming Population Decline and Revitalising Local Economies in September 2014 and Minister in Charge of the Dynamic Engagement of All Citizens in October 2015 in order to publicise his policy goals. In his August 2016 cabinet, for example, Abe created the post of Minister in Charge of Working Life Reform to promote his revamped goal in the field of employment policy.[282]

Abe's leadership style and capacity

Personal resource factors can also come into play alongside formal and informal power resources in determining the power of the prime minister and his executive office. The leadership capacity of the prime minister, particularly on policy matters, is an important determinant of just how effectively he can deploy the formal institutional structures available to him to pursue his preferred policy options and how he deals with potential opponents and rivals.

As Kaihara points out, 'Although political institutions can empower political actors, it is leadership that realizes the potential of political institutions.'[283] Mishima agrees that 'the nature of the prime ministership depends also on the capacity and orientation of its holder.'[284] Uchiyama also observes that 'the prime minister can use two types of resources to exercise power: institutional resources and personal resources.'[285] In other words, a supportive institutional environment alone is not sufficient for a Japanese prime minister to exercise strong leadership.[286] A prime minister must also be willing to harness the institutional infrastructure at his disposal and display skill in utilising 'the institutions placed at the disposal of executive authority to control the administration over which he presides'.[287] Here Koizumi and Abe are the standout performers.[288]

Leadership capacity is, in turn, influenced by personality, character and other individual attributes and character traits such as strength of policy convictions, ability to make judgements, knowledge of policies and ability to articulate them, the will to exercise power, political strategy skills, the capacity to garner public support and promote particular policies, and so on. So-called 'conviction politicians' such as Nakasone and Koizumi had a clear policy plan containing a set of concrete political objectives with Koizumi also bent on using to his political advantage the changed institutional environment in which he found himself.[289] Abe is another such politician, with a clear ideological agenda, including constitutional reform, and motivated to achieve a distinct set of policy objectives in relation to Japan's security posture as well as restoring the Japanese economy to growth on which his administration stands or falls. In policy areas such as these, he is a determined game changer focussed on pushing the various initiatives whereby his desired goals can be accomplished. As a result, his administration demonstrates a clear sense of purpose, which is one of its great strengths and which buttresses its executive power.[290]

While Abe has very strong ideas and opinions about what he wants to do and is industrious and articulate, he also proceeds strategically, which may require that he move cautiously and incrementally if he calculates that this approach will be more productive in terms of achieving his objectives. He is pragmatic and has a realistic understanding of what is possible politically at any point in time. His style is to set the policy agenda, define and articulate goals, choose the appropriate political strategies and then drive the policymaking process in the desired direction. Assisting this approach is Abe's use of sloganeering and the political 'marketing' of his ideas in order to persuade his party and the electorate to support his objectives. The three 'arrows' of Abenomics, for example, have been difficult to criticise because they hold out the hope that the Japanese economy will be restored to growth. Time after time, his electoral performance has been buoyed by the expectations of voters that these three arrows will deliver on their promise. Promoting these and other measures such as regional revitalisation has enabled the Abe administration skilfully to project the "'impression that it is doing something" and the "impression that it is looking and moving forward"'.[291] Such is the use of catchphrases by the Abe administration that some of its sloganeering borders on sheer propagandising. It appears designed to lead commentators by the nose with new jargon such as 'creating a society of dynamic engagement of all citizens', 'a society in which women can shine', or the 'new three arrows'.[292]

Abe himself actively engages with the media and is a dynamic public communicator as well as an articulate salesman of his government's policies. He deals with individual requests to appear on TV at his own discretion, rejecting the rule that interviews of the prime minister should be alternated between the national government-funded broadcaster NHK and national commercial networks. He also dines with media personnel including the executives of newspapers and TV stations in the interest of winning them over by building close relationships with them, which is exceptional for a Japanese prime minister.[293] At the same time, Abe is selective of the newspapers to whom he grants interviews, focussing mainly on right-wing outlets such as the *Sankei Shinbun* and *Yomiuri Shinbun*, even over and above the so-called Cabinet Press Club (commonly known as the 'Kantei Club'), but which can be relied on to express support for his actions and his government's policies, particularly in the security sphere.[294] Moreover, his administration has become synonymous with efforts to 'control the message' to the point of media intimidation.[295] Abe intervened in the personnel affairs of NHK, appointing Momii Katsuto as chairman in 2013, who was criticised for numerous problematic comments that were lenient towards the Abe administration,[296] and choosing four people to sit on the NHK's Board of Governors who were close to him and whose 'ability to make fair judgements in relation to the welfare of the public' had been called into question.[297] Abe also uses his close relations with NHK reporters to advance his own policy agenda.[298] The short 'doorstop' (*burasagari*) interviews, which used to be conducted twice daily by beat reporters assigned to the prime minister and began with the Koizumi administration and continued until they were abolished by the Noda Yoshihiko administration, have not been resurrected. They are now only granted when the Kantei deems it necessary.[299] Abe's preference is for choreographed appearances where there is little chance of having to improvise his answers or to respond to difficult questions from journalists.[300] Abe is also the first prime minister to take advantage of social media to get his message out.[301]

At times, Abe can show impatience with the political process, which he appears to regard as necessary more for the purpose of rubber-stamping and ratifying his decisions rather than for the purpose of democratic decision-making and demonstrating the democratic accountability of his government.

For this reason, he is not very mindful of the Diet, appearing to dislike question time in the Budget Committee, in which he can become verbally aggressive and speak at a rapid rate, and Diet discussions generally. As Mikuriya explains, 'he does not seem to be enthusiastic about "engaging in thorough deliberation". This is because once discussions hit a deadlock he is able to dismiss it as a "difference in opinion", and when push comes to shove he can use his power to stifle opposition.'[302] As a result, his political leadership style can appear top-down to the point of being autocratic. This reflects a broader shift in the LDP under Abe 'from a restrained political style that focuses on the formation of consensus to an authoritarian political style'.[303] To some, it amounts to 'cold totalitarianism that is quietly strengthening control from the top down'.[304]

Impact on the cabinet, cabinet ministers and the bureaucracy

The expansion and reinforcement of the powers of the prime ministerial executive under Abe have impacted directly on the powers and position of the cabinet in his administration. Fundamentally the prime ministerial executive has replaced the formal political executive as the supreme policymaking body. This is a system where '"the cabinet is a mainly residual organization" in policy-making, [and] ministers are "agents of the . . . prime minister's will"',[305] making the cabinet 'more an aggregation than a real institution'.[306] It is not a body of collective leadership but rather one committed to carrying out the prime minister's program.[307] Abe gives strong direction to the cabinet, and individual ministers are subordinate to the Kantei, which is dictating cabinet policy, with the ministers taking their orders from Abe and Suga. Such is the level of cabinet compliance with the prime ministerial executive that 'Even when the prime minister suddenly changes his mind, [the cabinet] just says, "Is that so? If the prime minister says so, then there is nothing we can do" and lets it go. They practically do not have their own opinion.'[308] The cabinet is simply a body for discussing and ratifying the prime minister's initiatives. As Curtis remarks, 'The cabinet is no longer a group of equals, each minister in effect being the CEO of his ministry with the prime minister serving as a kind of chairman of the board. This cabinet is Abe's cabinet. He demands loyalty and he gets it.'[309] In the Diet itself, Abe takes charge during Question Time, casting aside his ministers and confidently answering questions himself, particularly about difficult issues, thus controlling the debate.[310]

The balance of power has also shifted between the ministers and their ministries. No longer do cabinet ministers act merely as spokespersons for and purveyors of ministry interests. The traditional model whereby, as Kato puts it, 'ministers transform themselves into representatives of their ministries' interests and positions, regardless of their opinions as Diet members prior to assuming their portfolios',[311] no longer holds. Nor is the cabinet any longer an 'aggregation of such ministers'.[312] Bottom-up is now top-down: ministers are playing a more significant leadership role within their own ministries. At the same time, they are more likely to act as agents of the prime ministerial executive in imposing its will on the ministry's bureaucrats[313] because they are more subject to centralised direction and intervention by the prime minister and even by the Kantei, particularly the chief cabinet secretary. On occasions when ministers act as spokespersons and advocates for the policy positions and interests of the administrative organisations they head, they are far from successful, including in the case of the most powerful ministry of all – the MOF. When Finance Minister Asō, for example, tried to push the MOF line on continuing the hikes in the consumption tax after the first rise in April 2014, he consistently lost.

What is more, not only are the cabinet and its ministers subordinate to the prime ministerial executive but the ministers have become agents of the government in exercising strategic policy leadership over their ministries on the Kantei's behalf. This means that the bureaucrats have lost power relative to both their ministers and the prime ministerial executive. In relation to JA reform, for example, the MAFF ceded its role as a prominent policymaker, becoming just another negotiating party in the process of deciding outcomes on this issue without the authority that it used to possess over key policy decisions on agriculture. Its newfound position is symptomatic of the much broader weakening of the bureaucracy relative to the Kantei in the Abe administration. Economic policymaking in particular is controlled by the Kantei with Abe unwilling to leave things in the hands of the bureaucracy.[314]

Driving home this shift in power is the incorporation of ministers of state into the Cabinet Office and ministers in charge of (certain issues) into the Cabinet Secretariat,[315] organisations that make up the core government offices in the prime ministerial executive. In short, the prime ministerial executive has expanded to incorporate ministerial positions. For those who head ministries as well as discharging duties as ministers of state or ministers in charge (of certain issues), such an arrangement complicates their loyalties. The vast majority of Japanese ministers now carry these dual and triple responsibilities. For those ministers who are 'ministers without ministries', their loyalties are solely to the prime ministerial executive.

Impact on the ruling party

The prime ministerial executive's dominant position in policymaking also has significant ramifications for the LDP, both organisationally and in terms of the party's long-standing participation in policymaking as a separate, independent, decision-making body. With the prime ministerial executive using its authority to direct and decide national policy decisions on all important issues, the LDP's Executive Council and the PARC, as well as the *zoku giin* that inhabit the PARC committees, have undergone a relative decline in both their power and presence. The party's role in policymaking has shrunk in parallel with the increasing concentration of power in Kantei. The kind of policy decision-making that used to be shared between the party and the Kantei has now been replaced by a system of 'stronger Kantei and weaker party' (*kankō tōtei*) where, as Mikuriya describes it, 'the Kantei has become abnormally powerful while the party has all but lost its presence.'[316] Even the LDP's organisation seems to have been hollowed out, with an apparent decline in activities at the party's headquarters in Nagata-chō and fewer staff.[317] Given that the ruling party's impressive headquarters has had significant functional importance in terms of the policy activities conducted there, the hollowing out process is more than just symbolic. It used to provide LDP Diet members with opportunities to influence party policy deliberations and was the primary venue for the activities of the *zoku giin*.[318]

The prime ministerial executive's ascendancy is thus at risk of sidelining the LDP. The Japanese media describes this situation as an 'anomaly' that has emerged in the LDP's policymaking process whereby, under the banner of Kantei leadership, the traditional procedures and practices seen in the party before the LDP returned to power in 2012 are being bypassed or shortened on numerous occasions. Some party members are expressing fears that 'the party's involvement may weaken even further'.[319] Party policy committees no longer operate as an alternative, formalised locus of policymaking to the extent that they did. For example, the procedure for the outline of the bill for reforming the social security system bypassed the approval process of the PARC and Executive Council prior to the cabinet decision on the bill.[320] Similarly, as Tazaki points out, 'In relation to both the TPP and the approval of the exercise of the right of collective self-defence, the party confirmed the policy after it was set forth by the Kantei.'[321] The Kantei dominated the TPP policymaking process by leading, coordinating and 'imposing a strong layer of executive direction and control.'[322] Even former Prime Minister Koizumi rebuked Abe 'for forcing his policies on the people, failing to win over opposition politicians, and turning the ruling party into a bunch of yes men.'[323] Koizumi said, '"He is railroading everything. It seems he is in such haste", chiding Abe for not attempting to gain the support of the opposition DPJ for his controversial security legislation, and for the mood amongst the LDP Diet members'.[324]

However, unlike Koizumi, Abe, for all his exercise of executive power, has not entirely neglected the ruling party's screening system. The Abe-led executive might have changed its policymaking relationship with the LDP but the party's policy machinery still functions and so advance screening (*yotō shinsa*) still takes place. The party routinely discusses and scrutinises policy proposals from the Kantei and participates in policymaking as a unit that is separate and independent from the prime ministerial executive and thus still acts as a partial constraint on it.

Moreover, even though LDP Diet members, as members of the party organisation, exercise less autonomy and are subject to stronger incentives to follow the party leadership (LDP president and secretary-general), incentives remain for party members to act independently in the search for votes, funds and organisational backing in the quest to maximise electoral support. Abe and the Kantei can still not impose policies on the party over its strong opposition particularly in areas of entrenched vested interests such as agriculture. While the initiative for a whole host of policy reforms is coming from the prime ministerial executive, it still has to deal with the usual suspects attempting to exercise their influence – in some cases more successfully than others. The traditional players cannot, therefore, be written off completely, despite the much greater power of the prime minister and Kantei in the policymaking process.[325]

The key difference under Abe is that the prime ministerial executive is no longer necessarily bound by the advance screening-cum-prior-approval process. The ruling party may still be deeply involved in the policy process with the Executive Council continuing to act as the party's highest decision-making body responsible for preliminary deliberation on the budget and government bills.[326] Likewise, the PARC committees continue to scrutinise major government policies and legislation. However, these groups no longer work as powerfully and effectively to constrain executive power. The 25 Executive Council members and the key executives of the PARC's policy committees who are traditionally the leading *zoku* (or *zoku* 'bosses') remain the most influential representatives of specific industry and sectoral interests and the most authoritative politician-decision-makers *within the party*, but they no longer exercise blocking power over policy initiatives coming from the prime ministerial executive. In short, 'advance screening' no longer presages 'prior approval'. This means the ruling party is no longer a veto point, although coordination continues between the prime ministerial executive and the party, and deals are struck through a bargaining process. Confronted by the Kantei as 'the single strong body' (*Kantei ikkyō*), the LDP has been forced to shift its focus to negotiating conditions.[327] Its legendary power of veto has been reduced to the 'power to negotiate', where 'even opposing opinions only go as far as calling for a "cautious response".'[328] On the JA reform issue, for example, Nogami reports that 'the Kantei even cowed the *nōsui zoku* who were forced to keep quiet under Abe as the single strong figure [*Abe ikkyō*]'.[329]

Given these changes, it is inevitable that the alliance between ruling party members and the bureaucrats in policymaking has been eroded. In the past, the LDP was closely connected to the bureaucrats through the PARC. As Mikuriya points out, 'The PARC used to work hard to establish communication with the ministries and agencies, but now the Cabinet Secretariat is the leading body when it comes to solving [problems]. The activities of the LDP's PARC have become dull.'[330] Similarly, because politicians in the PARC could specialise in dealing with particular policy issues, ministries and agencies established close relationships with them, and bureaucrats worked on gaining the approval of the relevant politicians (*zoku giin*)'.[331] Indeed the *zoku giin* originally developed from the ministries' efforts to organisationally 'nurture' and 'use' politicians in order that their plans and opinions would be incorporated into policy.[332] The relationship was often cemented by a shared desire to defend a common set of vested interests.[333] However, this kind of 'lateral' or 'horizontal' connection is rapidly disappearing. The combination of the diminished influence of bureaucrats and the decline in the number and influence of *zoku giin* only serves further to reduce the LDP's power to control the Kantei.[334] Moreover, the loosening of ties between the bureaucrats and the *zoku giin* is slowly unravelling the 'policy triangles' that dominated policymaking in segregated policy domains.[335]

The party is even anticipating and accommodating the Kantei's position in advance. For example, Abe went on the offensive and got his way at several crucial junctures on tax reform. In August 2013, the chairman of the LDP's Research Commission on the Tax System Noda emphasised 'the prime minister's requests' in his speech to commission executives saying, 'Given the requests made by Prime Minister Abe . . . we will discuss the tax reforms that are needed to reinforce competitiveness.'[336] The timing was different from the commission's usual process of finalising the following fiscal year's Tax Reform Outline at the end of the year, but Abe's desire to push efforts to realise his 'growth strategy' required the commission to frontload part of their work.[337]

The Tax Commission was widely regarded as 'in a class of its own' in the sense that it singlehandedly dealt with tax issues, and in many cases, its decision was adopted as the government's decision.[338] It had a reputation for jealously guarding its autonomy over tax policy and such was its authority over the delicate process of coordinating the complex interests of related industries and party support organisations that 'even the prime minister could not interfere'.[339] Under Abe, however, it began increasingly to show consideration for the Kantei's views and requests, reinforcing the impression that its influence was declining.[340] In late 2013, for example, it was led around by the nose by the Kantei on both the consumption and corporate tax issues, being forced to accommodate both postponing the tax hike due in April 2014 and lowering the corporate tax rate.[341]

Later, with both the prime minister and Minister of State for Economic and Fiscal Policy and Minister in Charge of Economic Revitalisation Amari repeatedly pushing for a cut in the corporate tax rate, the commission agreed to implement the tax cut in December 2014. The Tax Reform Outline for fiscal 2015 reflected that decision.[342] Noda, as chairman of the commission, had been arguing that reducing the real corporate tax rate required an alternative revenue source, and that the consumption tax hike to 10 per cent due to take place in October 2015, 'must be carried out'.[343] In fact, both the MOF and the commission had always insisted on 'revenue neutrality' between tax rises and tax cuts.[344] However, the prime minister first announced a postponement of the consumption tax increase, then when the Tax Reform Outline was completed, it included the claims made by the Kantei, METI and the Amari who all emphasised growth (meaning no tax hike).[345] Previously, it had been customary for the content of the Tax Reform Outline decided by the ruling party to be finalised as it was.[346] However, because the prime minister had successfully gained a mandate in the December 2014 election to postpone the consumption tax increase and continue with his 'Abenomics' growth-oriented program, the commission could not very well oppose the prime minister's policy of cutting the corporate tax rate and prioritising tax cuts. This meant that the advocates of fiscal discipline in the commission had to take a back seat in the face of the Kantei's wishes in a situation where, once again, 'the prime minister was the single strong entity' (*shushō ikkyō*).[347] After the Tax Reform Outline was decided on 30 December 2014, Noda, when asked whether the commission's authority had been lost, replied, 'It may be because I am powerless'.[348] What essentially broke down the ramparts of the commission was the prime minister's use of his power to dissolve the Lower House and his campaigning on the basis of a postponement of the second consumption tax hike and his growth strategy centred on a corporate tax cut. The Kantei even suggested the possibility of the LDP's not officially endorsing Noda in the election, which shook up the whole commission.[349] Noda said, 'We are not negotiating with the prime minister. He is the prime minister and party leader, so we are working under him', denying that he was engaged in a confrontation with the Kantei.[350] The commission later appointed Amari to its informal 'inner circle' of key executives in order to reinforce its connection with the Kantei.[351]

Such developments reveal the extent of the structural changes to the traditional *seifu-yotō* policymaking system. To the extent that negotiations and bargaining over policies continue between the Abe-led executive and the ruling party, a dual structure of 'government-party' policymaking remains, but its composition has changed and the balance of power has shifted in favour of the Abe-led executive.[352] The model is no longer 'LDP *zoku*-relevant ministry' as the two most powerful players and veto points. It is party-prime ministerial executive, with the latter dominating the government side to the virtual exclusion of other players.

A key aspect of the Abe prime ministership is thus the way he has managed to build and sustain centralised control over both the bureaucracy and the party.[353] This structural change has also altered the direction of policy from bottom-up to top-down.

Notes

1 'Abe Aims at Strong PM office, Plans Tech-led Growth Strategy', *The Nikkei Weekly*, 2 October 2006, p. 1.
2 'Abe Models Office on White House', *The Nikkei Weekly*, 2 October 2006, p. 2.
3 Uchiyama, Yū, Nihon seiji no akutā to seisaku kettei patān' ['Actors and Policymaking Patterns in Japanese Politics'], *Kikan Seisaku Keiei Kenkyū*, Vol. 3, Mitsubishi UFJ Research and Consulting, 2010, www.murc.jp/english/think_tank/quarterly_journal/qj1003_01.pdf, p. 14.
4 Tazaki, Shirō, *Abe kantei no shōtai* [*The Truth about Abe's Kantei*], Tokyo, Kōdansha, 2014, p. 51.
5 Tazaki, *Abe kantei*, p. 55.
6 Abe did staff a special office in charge of policy planning with five bureaucrats who shared his views in an attempt to circumvent the vertical divisions amongst the ministries. This group worked directly to him, but his special advisers played the leading role in key areas of policy.
7 Mikuriya, Takashi, *Abe seiken wa hontō ni tsuyoi no ka* [*Is the Abe Administration Actually Strong?*], Tokyo, PHP Kenkyūjo, 2015, p. 43.
8 Tazaki, *Abe kantei*, p. 51.
9 Mikuriya, *Abe seiken*, p. 42.
10 Takenaka, Heizō, 'Abe seiken no seisaku kettei purosesu', www.jcer.or.jp/column/takenaka/index565.html.
11 Sugiura, Nobuhiko, *JA ga kawareba Nihon no nōgyō wa tsuyoku naru* [*Japan's Agricultural Industry Will Become Stronger If JA Changes*], Tokyo, Discover21, 2015, p. 31.
12 'Ano iwakutsuki no giin ga jūyō posuto de fukkatsu!' ['That Diet Member with a Past Was Revived in an Important Post!'], *President Online*, 15 June 2015, http://president.jp/articles/-/15367.
13 Tazaki, *Abe kantei*, pp. 62–63.
14 Mikuriya, *Abe seiken*, pp. 43, 44.
15 Mikuriya, *Abe seiken*, p. 42.
16 Andō Takeshi, 'Nōkyō kaikaku, "kyūtenkai" no wake, Kizukeba "shimensoka" no JA chūō soshiki' ['The Reason for the "Rapid Developments" in the Reforms to the JA, The JA's Central Organisations Found Themselves "Forsaken by

Everyone'"], *Nikkei Business Online*, 20 May 2014, http://business.nikkeibp.
co.jp/article/opinion/20140519/264917/.

17 'Kantei shudō ga irokoku, 16 nendo yosanan, Saninsen e gyōkai hairyo' ['Strong
Characteristics of Kantei's Leadership, Budget Proposal for Fiscal 2016
Shows Consideration for Industries in Preparation for Upper House Elec-
tion'], *Nihon Keizai Shinbun*, 25 December 2015, www.nikkei.com/article/
DGXLZO95520470V21C15A2EA1000/.

18 'Naikaku kanbō no kenkyū (jō), Kantei shūken shōchō wa teashi, Hatarakikata
kaikaku, tai Bei kōshō . . . Omo na seisaku dokusen, "chōsei dake" ima wa
mukashi' ['A Study of the Cabinet Secretariat (Part 1): Concentration of Power
in the Kantei with the Ministries at their Beck and Call, Work Style Reform,
Negotiations with the US . . . Kantei Monopolises Major Policies, "Only Working on Coordination" Is Something of the Past'], *Nihon Keizai Shinbun*, 18 April
2017, p. 4.

19 Curtis, Gerald L., *Japan Update Speech*, Paper delivered to the Japan Update
Conference, Crawford School, Australian National University, Canberra, 21st
September 2016, p. 6.

20 Mikuriya, *Abe seiken*, p. 111.

21 '"Abe ikkyō no bōsō ni burēki o. Ryōshiki aru kokkai giin no hataraki sasaeru
seron zukuri e, jūyō na JA gurūpu no kesshūryoku' ['Stop the Recklessness of
"Abe as the Single Strong Figure". The JA Group's Uniting Power Is Important
to Create Public Opinion That Supports the Work of Diet Members Who Have
a Conscience'], *Nōsei Undō Jānaru*, No. 119, February 2015, p. 16.

22 Machidori, *Shushō seiji*, p. 99.

23 See also Heffernan, Richard, *Presidentialization in the United Kingdom*, https://
ecpr.eu/Filestore/PaperProposal/9c85aa57-e9c7-45b9-bd92-2eb41282e737.
pdf, p. 2.

24 'Naikaku kanbō no kenkyū (jō), p. 4.

25 'Kokka kōmuin no teiin (Heisei 13 nendo-28 nendo)' ['Number of National
Public Servants (FY 2001-FY 2016)'], Cabinet Secretariat website, www.cas.
go.jp/jp/gaiyou/jimu/jinjikyoku/files/h280401_teiin.xlsx; 'Naikaku kanbō no
kenkyū (jō)', p. 4.

26 Makihara, Izuru, 'Seisaku kettei ni okeru shushō kantei no yakuwari' ['The
Role of the Kantei in Making Policy'], *Nippon.com*, 27 June 2013, www.nippon.
com/ja/features/c00408/.

27 Asano, Takaaki, 'Abenomikusu o sasaeru mittsu no seisaku kaigi' ['The Three
Policy Councils That Support Abenomics'], *The Tokyo Foundation*, 2 July
2013 (Reproduced from *Bijinesu Hōmu*, July 2013 edition), www.tkfd.or.jp/
research/project/news.php?id=1158.

28 These were the Headquarters for Japan's Economic Revitalisation, the Industrial
Competitiveness Council, the Regulatory Reform Council, the Headquarters
for the Promotion of Administrative Reform, the Ministerial Council on the
Promotion of Japan as a Tourism-Oriented Country, the Headquarters on the
Abduction Issue, the Advisory Panel on Reconstruction of the Legal Basis
for Security, Advisory Council on the Establishment of a National Security
Council, the Examination Committee on the Response to the Terrorist Attack
on Japanese Persons in Algeria, the Education Rebuilding Implementation
Council, the Ministerial Meeting on Strategy relating to Infrastructure Export
and Economic Cooperation, the Headquarters for Promoting Decentralisation

Reform, the Forum for Promoting the Active Participation by Young People and Women, the Advisory Council on the Protection etc. of Japanese Residents and Enterprises Overseas and the Council of Senior Vice-Ministers etc. on the Monitoring of Financing etc. for Small and Medium Enterprises. This information was obtained from 'Omo na honbu-kaigitai' ['Main Headquarters and Council Bodies'], in *Shushō kantei* [*Prime Minister of Japan and His Cabinet*], www.kantei.go.jp/jp/singi/index.html.

29 The Regulatory Reform Promotion Council held its first meeting on 12 September 2016.

30 Asano, 'Abenomikusu o sasaeru mittsu no seisaku kaigi', www.tkfd.or.jp/research/project/news.php?id=1158.

31 Asano, 'Abenomikusu o sasaeru mittsu no seisaku kaigi', www.tkfd.or.jp/research/project/news.php?id=1158.

32 Tazaki, *Abe kantei*, p. 224.

33 Prime Minister of Japan and His Cabinet, *Press Conference by the Chief Cabinet Secretary*, Tuesday, 7 January 2014 (AM), http://japan.kantei.go.jp/tyoukanpress/201401/07_a.html.

34 'Naikaku kanbō no kenkyū (jō)', p. 4.

35 These figures were calculated from lists in 'Omo na honbu-kaigitai', www.kantei.go.jp/jp/singi/index.html.

36 Abe Shinzō o kangaeru kai, *Abe Shinzō to wa nanimono ka?* [*Who Is Shinzō Abe?*], Tokyo, Makino Shuppan, 2015, p. 36.

37 Asano, 'Abenomikusu o sasaeru mittsu no seisaku kaigi', www.tkfd.or.jp/research/project/news.php?id=1158.

38 'Kantei shudō seiji ni, tō, kokkai ga sonzaikan o hakki' ['The Party and the Diet Exert A Strong Presence in Kantei-led Politics'], *Nōsei Undō Jānaru*, No. 112, December 2013, p. 17.

39 Hanatani, Mie, '"Kantei ikkyō" no iroai tsuyomaru keizai seisaku no kettei' ['Kantei Dominates Economic Policymaking under the Abe Administration'], *Ekonomisuto*, 10 May 2016, p. 25.

40 Shiozaki, Yasuhisa, 'Changes in the Japanese Policymaking Process', in Thomas E. Mann and Takeshi Sasaki (eds), *Governance for a New Century: Japanese Challenges, American Experience*, Tokyo, Japan Center for International Exchange, 2002, p. 61.

41 See *Nihon keizai zaisei honbu meibo* [*Headquarters for Japan's Economic Revitalisation Membership List*], 1 September 2016, www.kantei.go.jp/jp/singi/keizaisaisei/pdf/meibo.pdf.

42 Asano, 'Abenomikusu o sasaeru mittsu no seisaku kaigi', www.tkfd.or.jp/research/project/news.php?id=1158.

43 Asano, 'Abenomikusu o sasaeru mittsu no seisaku kaigi', www.tkfd.or.jp/research/project/news.php?id=1158.

44 Minami, Akira, 'Kasumigaseki no meishu, Zaimushō kara Keisanshō e Shushō sokkin ni shusshinsha' ['The Ministry of Economy, Trade and Industry Wrests Kasumigaseki Crown from the Ministry of Finance, Supplying Bureaucrats for Positions Close to Abe'], *Asahi Shinbun Digital*, 28 February 2017, www.asahi.com/articles/ASK2S43XWK2SUTFK012.html.

45 'Ano iwakutsuki no giin', http://president.jp/articles/-/15367.

46 '[Kinkyū intabyū Keizai hyōronka Uchihashi Katsuto shi ni kiku (jō)] "Nōkyō kaikaku" o kiru, hihan seishin tsuyome taikōjiku o' ['[Emergency Interview

with Economic Critic Uchihashi Katsuto (Part 1)] Criticising the "Agricultural Cooperative Reform"; Strengthen Critical Mindset and Build Foundation for Opposition'], *JAcom*, 30 November 2016, www.jacom.or.jp/nousei/closeup/2016/161130-31506.php.

47 The list is available at Liberal Democratic Party of Japan, *Official English Translations for LDP Officials and Party Organs*, www.jimin.jp/english/profile/english/.

48 Heffernan, *Presidentialization in the United Kingdom*, p. 26.

49 Abe Shinzō o kangaeru kai, *Abe Shinzō to wa nanimono ka?*, p. 84.

50 Abe quoted in Tazaki, *Abe kantei*, pp. 166–167.

51 Tazaki, *Abe kantei*, p. 167.

52 'Tanigaki kokete haran, Abe shushō ga Ima kangaete Iru "gyōten jinji"' ['Tanigaki's Fall Causes a Commotion; The "Surprise Personnel Decisions" That Prime Minister Abe Is Thinking about Right Now'], *Shūkan Gendai*, 6 August 2016, p. 76. See also below.

53 'Tanigaki kokete haran', p. 76.

54 As Iio explains, members of the Executive Council 'are selected based on consideration of balance between regions and factions, and often influential members who happen not to hold any other posts are selected.' *Nihon no tōchi kōzō*, p. 84.

55 'Menkai ōi aite wa? Abe shushō no 4 nenkan, dēta de kaibō' ['Who Meets Abe Most? An Analysis of Data on Abe's Four Years as Prime Minister'], *Nihon Keizai Shinbun*, 29 January 2017, www.nikkei.com/article/DGXLZO12255640Y7A120C1TZJ000/.

56 '"Asō shi wa 'Abe sōri mo kodoku nanda' to" Kawamura giun iinchō' ['Lower House Steering Committee Chairman Kawamura Says, "Asō Said That 'Prime Minister Abe Is Isolated'"'], *Asahi Shinbun Digital*, 4 June 2016, www.asahi.com/articles/ASJ646589J64UTFK00D.html.

57 'Naikaku kaizō e omowaku kōsaku, Suga, Asō shi ryūnin e, Kokkaku iji' ['Intentions Intertwine Ahead of Cabinet Reshuffle, Suga and Asō to Keep Posts, Administration's Framework to Be Maintained'], *Nihon Keizai Shinbun*, 26 July 2016, www.nikkei.com/article/DGXLASDE25H09_V20C16A7PP8000/.

58 Tazaki, *Abe kantei*, p. 29.

59 This is the position of principal secretary (*shuseki hishokan*), or secretary in charge of political affairs (*seimu tantō shushō hishokan*), viz., Abe's political secretary.

60 Tazaki, *Abe kantei*, p. 29. In fact, Abe has seven executive secretaries including Imai. The others are recruits from the public service and are in charge of administrative affairs.

61 Imai and Ministry of Economy, Trade and Industry (METI) Administrative Vice-Minister, Sugawara Ikurō, are known as 'Abe's "METI mafia".' Toshikawa, Takao, 'Upper House Election Prospects: Why No "Double Election" This Year', *The Oriental Economist Report*, Vol. 84, No. 6, June 2016, p. 4.

62 Minami, 'Kasumigaseki no meishu', www.asahi.com/articles/ASK2S43XWK2SUTFK012.html.

63 Tazaki, *Abe kantei*, p. 32

64 Tazaki, *Abe kantei*, p. 35.

65 Tazaki, *Abe kantei*, p. 42.

66 Tazaki, *Abe kantei*, p. 243.

67 Tazaki, *Abe kantei*, p. 219.
68 Tazaki, *Abe kantei*, p. 42.
69 '[Tantō chokugen] Hagiuda Kōichi kanbō fukuchōkan, "Abe ikkyō" nani ga waruin desu ka' ['[Point-blank comment] Deputy Chief Cabinet Secretary Kōichi Hagiuda Asks What Is Wrong with Abe Seizing "Unrivalled Control"'], *Sankei Shinbun*, 24 April 2017, p. 5.
70 See also below.
71 'Naikaku kanbō no kenkyū (chū) Kakushō kara ēsu kanryō, Kantei no ikō, jinsoku ni jitsugen' ['A Study of the Cabinet Secretariat (Part 2): Bringing in Ace Bureaucrats from Various Ministries to Swiftly Realise What the Kantei Wants'], *Nihon Keizai Shinbun*, 19 April 2017, p. 4.
72 Tazaki, *Abe kantei*, p. 58.
73 See Sakano, *The Presidentialization of Politics*, p. 22.
74 Tazaki, *Abe kantei*, p. 57.
75 Abe Shinzō o kangaeru kai, *Abe Shinzō to wa nanimono ka?*, p. 88.
76 Hanatani, '"Kantei ikkyō"', p. 25. See also below.
77 Abe Shinzō o kangaeru kai, *Abe Shinzō to wa nanimono ka?*, p. 88.
78 Tazaki, *Abe kantei*, p. 57.
79 Tazaki, *Abe kantei*, pp. 219–220. See also below.
80 'Shushō sasaeru "kuroko" goninshū hosakan, jitsumu jūshi no jogenyaku, gaikō, kōhō . . . senmon bunya ikasu' ['The Five "Unsung Heroes" Who Support Abe, Advisors' Emphasis on Practical Work, Effectively Use Specialised Skills in diplomacy, PR etc.'], *Nihon Keizai Shinbun*, 17 June 2016, www.nikkei.com/article/DGKKZO03723970X10C16A6EAC000/.
81 Takenaka, 'Abe seiken no seisaku kettei purosesu', www.jcer.or.jp/column/takenaka/index565.html.
82 Takayasu, 'The Pressures of Change', www.nippon.com/en/features/c00410/.
83 Hanatani, '"Kantei ikkyō"', p. 25.
84 Abe Shinzō o kangaeru kai, *Abe Shinzō to wa nanimono ka?*, p. 36; 'Shushō no shinanyaku Hamada kyōju ga GPIF kabu tōshi "ōzon" no gyōten hatsugen' ['Prime Minister's Mentor, Professor Hamada Makes Shocking Comment on GPIF Stock Investments Resulting in Potential "Major Losses"'], *Nikkan Gendai*, 19 January 2016 www.nikkan-gendai.com/articles/view/news/173564.
85 Abe Shinzō o kangaeru kai, *Abe Shinzō to wa nanimono ka?*, p. 96.
86 'Abe shushō no keizai seisaku burēn, Suisu taishi ni irei no tenshutsu Honda Etsurō naikaku kanbō sanyo' ['Prime Minister Abe's Economic Policy Brains and Special Advisor to the Cabinet Etsurō Honda Appointed as Ambassador to Switzerland in Exceptional Personnel Decision'], *Sankei Shinbun*, 11 March 2016, www.sankei.com/politics/news/160311/plt1603110032-n1.html.
87 Abe Shinzō o kangaeru kai, *Abe Shinzō to wa nanimono ka?*, p. 97.
88 Prime Minister of Japan and His Cabinet, *Press Conference*, http://japan.kantei.go.jp/tyoukanpress/201401/07_a.html.
89 Mikuriya, *Abe seiken*, pp. 45–46.
90 Hanatani, '"Kantei ikkyō"', p. 25.
91 According to one government official, it was impossible to operate in Kasumigaseki if one incurred Sugita's displeasure. 'Naikaku kanbō no kenkyū (chū)', p. 4.
92 'Naikaku kanbō no kenkyū (chū)', p. 4.
93 'Menkai ōi aite wa?', www.nikkei.com/article/DGXLZO12255640Y7A120C1TZJ000/.

94 'Movers of Abe's Diplomacy', *Sentaku*, 11 February 2013, www.japantimes. co.jp/opinion/2013/02/11/commentary/japan-commentary/movers-of-abes-diplomacy/.

95 Various comments have been made about Abe's level of trust in Suga such as, Suga is 'the one who is most trusted by Prime Minister Abe' and 'No one is as trustworthy as Suga for Prime Minister Abe'. Abe Shinzō o kangaeru kai, *Abe Shinzō to wa nanimono ka?*, p. 84; and Abe 'also trusts Suga and fully entrusts him with domestic issues'. Tazaki, *Abe kantei*, p. 189. See also Mikuriya, *Abe seiken*, p. 45; Tazaki, *Abe kantei*, p. 42.

96 'Abe no saidai no seiteki wa "Suga Yoshihide"', p. 49.

97 Mikuriya, *Abe seiken*, p. 48.

98 Mikuriya, *Abe seiken*, p. 58.

99 Toshikawa, 'Upper House Election Prospects', p. 5.

100 'Hatsu taidan dokusen 70 pun, Suga *kanbō chōkan* Toranpu daitōryō no tsuittā, keizai seisaku wa tegowai, Nikai kajichō Koike san wa wareware to hantai no koto o suru to omotte chōdo ii, Toranpu daitōryō, Koike gekijō, postuo Abe, tennō taii, kaisan senryaku, "amakudari" o katatta' ['First 70-minute Exclusive Joint Interview, Chief Cabinet Secretary Suga: "President Trump's Twitter and Economic Policies Are Tough Issues", Secretary-General Nikai: "You Can Assume that Koike Will Do the Opposite of What We Do", Discussions on President Trump, the Koike Theatre, Post-Abe, Emperor's Abdication, Dissolution Strategy, and "amakudari"'], *Shūkan Asahi*, 17 February 2017, p. 27.

101 'Abe no saidai no seiteki wa "Suga Yoshihide", "Shukun to chūshin", Chikara kankei ga gyakuten suru hi' ['Abe's Biggest Political Rival Is "Yoshihide Suga", "Master and Loyal Retainer", The Day the Power Relationship Becomes Reversed'], *Sentaku*, November 2015, p. 50.

102 Abe Shinzō o kangaeru kai, *Abe Shinzō to wa nanimono ka?*, p. 84.

103 Mikuriya, *Abe seiken*, p. 217.

104 'Suga *kanbō chōkan* zaishoku saichō ni 1290 nichi, Fukuda Yasuo shi o nuku' ['Suga Becomes the Longest Serving Chief Cabinet Secretary at 1290 Days, Breaks Yasuo Fukuda's Record'], *Asahi Shinbun*, 7 July 2016, p. 4.

105 Suzuki, Tetsuo, '*Kaibō seikai kīman* Suga Yoshihide *kanbō chōkan* Kasumigaseki ni nirami o kikasu "jinji" to seiken sasaeru "shoku ni tessuru"' ['*Dissecting Key Political Figures* Chief Cabinet Secretary Yoshihide Suga: Use "Personnel Affairs" to Exert Pressure Against Kasumigaseki and "Devote All Efforts to the Job" to Support the Administration'], Zakzak by *Yūkan Fuji*, 13 August 2016, www.zakzak.co.jp/society/politics/news/20160813/plt1608131000002-n1.htm.

106 Suzuki, '*Kaibō seikai kīman*', www.zakzak.co.jp/society/politics/news/20160813/plt1608131000002-n1.htm.

107 Iizuka, Keiko and Smith, Sheila A., 'Who Is Shinzo Abe?', Council on Foreign Relations, CFT Events, 15 May 2015, www.cfr.org/japan/shinzo-abe/p36523.

108 Makihara, 'Abe's enforcer', www.nippon.com/en/currents/d00135/.

109 Makihara, 'Abe's enforcer', www.nippon.com/en/currents/d00135/.

110 Makihara, 'Abe's enforcer', www.nippon.com/en/currents/d00135/.

111 Mikuriya, *Abe seiken*, p. 52.

112 Mikuriya, *Abe seiken*, pp. 52–53.

113 Makihara, 'Seisaku kettei', www.nippon.com/ja/features/c00408/.

114 Mikuriya, *Abe seiken*, p. 66. See also below.

115 Mikuriya, *Abe seiken*, p. 67.
116 'Shushō kantei no media kōryaku jutsu', pp. 48–51.
117 Takayasu, 'The Pressures of Change', www.nippon.com/en/features/c00410/.
118 'Naikaku kanbō no kenkyū (jō)', p. 4.
119 'Kokka kōmuin no teiin (Heisei 13 nendo-28 nendo)' ['Number of National Public Servants (FY 2001-FY 2016)'] Cabinet Secretariat website, www.cas. go.jp/jp/gaiyou/jimu/jinjikyoku/files/h280401_teiin.xlsx; 'Naikaku kanbō no kenkyū (jō)', p. 4.
120 See also below.
121 Makihara, 'The Role of the Kantei in Making Policy', www.nippon.com/en/ features/c00408/. See also below.
122 Mikuriya, *Abe seiken*, p. 59.
123 Mikuriya, *Abe seiken*, p. 48.
124 Makihara, 'Abe's enforcer', www.nippon.com/en/currents/d00135//
125 'Abe Shinzō ga kage no saishō Suga Yoshihide no "hanran" ni obie hajimeta, "Mō iiyo. Ore wa tsukareta"' ['Shinzō Abe Has Started to Become Scared of the "Rebellion" of Yoshihide Suga, the Prime Minister Behind the Curtain, "I Give Up. I'm Tired."'], *Shūkan Bijinesu*, 30 April edition, pp. 36–40, via *Gendai Bijinesu*, 25 April 2016, http://gendai.ismedia.jp/articles/-/48499. Curtis made a similar observation about Chief Cabinet Secretary Fukuda during Koizumi's administration saying that Fukuda had 'emerged as the key figure in coordinating the policy process, in some ways making him more powerful than the prime minister himself'. *Institutional Change*, p. 8.
126 Mikuriya, *Abe seiken*, p. 48.
127 This particular episode is detailed in Yoshida, Reiji, 'Nishimuro Tapped to Take over Japan Post, Move Shows LDP Coalition's Bid for Influence', *The Japan Times*, 11 May 2013, www.japantimes.co.jp/news/2013/05/11/business/ nishimuro-tapped-to-take-over-japan-post/#.WAnCXISRC-I; and Makihara, 'Abe's Enforcer', www.nippon.com/en/currents/d00135/.
128 Makihara, 'Abe's Enforcer', www.nippon.com/en/currents/d00135/.
129 Tazaki, *Abe kantei*, p. 62.
130 Tazaki, *Abe kantei*, p. 64.
131 Abe Shinzō o kangaeru kai, *Abe Shinzō to wa nanimono ka?*, p. 89.
132 Mikuriya, *Abe seiken*, p. 49.
133 'Naikaku kanbō no kenkyū (ge): Shōchō jinji mo kantei shudō', Kado na sontaku umu kenen' ['A Study of the Cabinet Secretariat (Part 3): Kantei Controls Appointments in the Ministries, Concern That It May Lead to Excessively Surmising the Kantei's Intentions'], *Nihon Keizai Shinbun*, 21 April 2017, p. 4.
134 Mikuriya, *Abe seiken*, p. 49.
135 Abe Shinzō o kangaeru kai, *Abe Shinzō to wa nanimono ka?*, p. 89.
136 'Chūō shōchō jinji kantei shudō ga teichaku, Josei kanbu zōka "2 kaikyū tokushin"' "Ishuku" kenen mo' ['Kantei Leadership over Personnel Affairs in Central Government Ministries and Agencies Established, Increase in Female Executives and "Promotion by Two Ranks", Concern over "Intimidation"'], *Yomiuri Shinbun*, 15 June 2016, p. 4.
137 '[Seiji no genba] Chōki seiken no tenbō (4) Jinji nigiri kanryō o "saiten"' ['[The Grassroots of Politics] The Long-Term Administration's Vision (4) "Grade" Bureaucrats by Controlling Personnel Decisions'], *Yomiuri Shinbun*, 2 December 2016, p. 4.

78 *Power in the second Abe administration*

138 'Naikaku kanbō no kenkyū (ge)', p. 4.
139 Mikuriya, *Abe seiken*, pp. 49–50.
140 Mikuriya, *Abe seiken*, p. 50.
141 'Chūō shōchō', p. 4.
142 Ogawa, Mayumi, 'Koizumi Shinjirō Jimin nōrin bukaichō "hitoyose panda" o sotsugyō? Nōgyō kaikaku de shuwan apīru, Shūi kara "dekirēsu" no kageguchi mo . . .' ['Has LDP Agriculture and Forestry Division Director Koizumi Shinjirō Become More Than a "Crowd Puller"? Koizumi Emphasises His Skills in Relation to Agricultural Reform, Some People Talk Behind His Back That It Was a "Fixed Game". . .'], *Sankei News*, 2 December 2016, www.sankei.com/premium/news/161202/prm1612020007-n1.html. See also below.
143 'Chūō shōchō', p. 4. See also George Mulgan, 'Loosening the Ties That Bind', pp. 221–246. See also below.
144 'Naikaku kanbō no kenkyū (ge)', p. 4.
145 '[Seiji no genba] Chōki seiken no tenbō (4)', p. 4.
146 '[Seiji no genba] Chōki seiken no tenbō (4)', p. 4.
147 Toshikawa, Takao, 'MOF Loses Tax Fight to Abe: Kantei Asserts Its Power', *The Oriental Economist Report*, Vol. 84, No. 1, January 2016, p. 4.
148 Taoka, Shunji, 'Chūgoku gunkan no setsuzoku suiiki kōkō e no kōgi wa jibun no kubi o shimeru kōi' ['The Government Is Digging Their Own Grave by Protesting the Chinese Naval Vessels Entering the Contiguous Zone'], *Diamond Online*, 16 June 2016, http://diamond.jp/articles/-/93104.
149 'Chūō shōchō jinji kantei shudō ga teichaku', p. 4.
150 'Naikaku kanbō no kenkyū (ge)', p. 4.
151 Toshikawa, 'MOF Loses Tax Fight', p. 5.
152 'Naikaku kanbō no kenkyū (ge)', p. 4.
153 Mikuriya, *Abe seiken*, p. 55.
154 Mikuriya, *Abe seiken*, p. 56, 57.
155 Makihara, 'Seisaku kettei', www.nippon.com/ja/features/c00408/.
156 Mikuriya, *Abe seiken*, p. 59.
157 Tazaki, *Abe kantei*, p. 185.
158 Tazaki, *Abe kantei*, p. 31.
159 Aihara, Ryō and Oyamada, Kenji, '(Jiji Kokukoku) Nōkyō kaikaku, seiken oshikiru, Zenchū no kengen, ōhaba shukushō' ['(Moment to Moment) Administration Overcomes Opposition to JA Reform, JA's Authority Significantly Reduced'], *Asahi Shinbun Digital*, 10 February 2015, http://digital.asahi.com/articles/DA3S11593742.html.
160 Iida, Yasumichi, *JA kaitai – 1000 man kumiaiin no meiun* [*Dissolution of JA – The Fate of the 10 Million Members*], Tokyo, Tōyō Keizai Shinpōsha, 2015, p. 130.
161 'Nōkyō kaikaku, ganban kuzushi e kantei no shūnen, Saga chijisen no haiboku no bane' ['JA Reform, The Kantei's Tenacity in Undermining the Bedrock, The Kantei Sprung Back from Defeat in the Saga Gubernatorial Election'], *Nihon Keizai Shinbun*, 10 February 2015, www.nikkei.com/article/DGXLASFS09H7E_Z00C15A2EA2000/.
162 Aihara and Oyamada, '(Jiji kokukoku) Nōkyō kaikaku', http://digital.asahi.com/articles/DA3S11593742.html.
163 Tazaki, Shirō, 'JA Zenchū ga enjita Zaimushō no ni no mai, Abe kantei ni "sotobori senpō" wa tsūjizu' ['The Central Union of Agricultural Cooperatives

Followed in the Footsteps of the Ministry of Finance, The "Tactic of Encircling the Kantei" Did Not Work'], *Gendai Business*, 9 February 2015, http://gendai. ismedia.jp/articles/-/42013.

164 Kishi, Hiroyuki, 'Nōgyō kaikaku wa doko made jitsugen suru ka' ['To What Extent Will Agricultural Reforms Be Realised?'], *Diamond Online*, No. 265, 23 May 2014, http://diamond.jp/articles/-/53453. See also below.

165 Kishi, 'Nōgyō kaikaku', http://diamond.jp/articles/-/53453.

166 Tazaki, 'JA Zenchū', http://gendai.ismedia.jp/articles/-/42013

167 Iida, *JA kaitai*, p. 123.

168 Iida, *JA kaitai*, p. 118.

169 'Shushō, jizen no jūryōkyū kiyō, Jimin kanjichō ni Nikai shi, "Sōsai ninki enchō e no fuseki" to no mikata ['Prime Minister Settles for Second Best Heavyweight Nikai as LDP Secretary-General, Views That It Is a "Preparatory Step for Extending His Term of Office as LDP Leader"'], *Nihon Keizai Shinbun*, 2 August 2016, p. 4. Nikai supported Abe's bid for the presidency of the LDP in September 2015. See also below.

170 'Abe no saidai no seiteki wa "Suga Yoshihide"', pp. 48–50.

171 'Hatsu taidan dokusen 70 pun', p. 27.

172 'Abe no saidai no seiteki wa "Suga Yoshihide"', p. 48

173 'Abe no saidai no seiteki wa "Suga Yoshihide"', p. 49.

174 Toshikawa, 'MOF Loses Tax Fight', p. 4.

175 Toshikawa, 'MOF Loses Tax Fight', p. 4.

176 Toshikawa, 'MOF Loses Tax Fight', p. 5.

177 Tazaki, *Abe kantei*, p. 211.

178 Toshikawa, 'MOF Loses Tax Fight', p. 4.

179 'Kantei shudō ga irokoku', www.nikkei.com/article/DGXLZO95520470V21C 15A2EA1000/.

180 'Kantei shudō ga irokoku', www.nikkei.com/article/DGXLZO95520470V21C 15A2EA1000/.

181 Hanatani, '"Kantei ikkyō"', p. 25. In July 2016, however, the prime minister accepted the MOF's proposal for funding the government's economic stimulus package worth ¥28.1 trillion through a massive injection of funds from the Fiscal Investment and Loan Program (FILP) rather than issuing new government bonds. 'Abe's Unorthodox Policies Rooted in Distrust of Finance Ministry, BOJ', *Nikkei Asian Review*, 16 October 2016.

182 'Kigyō no nōchi shoyū nin'yō, Gōin na kanwa wa kōka ni gimon, Nōka fushinkan, dashishiburi ni hakusha mo' ['Effects of Forcibly Relaxing Regulations to Allow Farmland Ownership by Companies Questionable, It May Breed Distrust among Farmers and Encourage Them to Hold Onto Their Land'], *Sankei Shinbun*, 3 March 2016, p. 11.

183 Mikuriya, *Abe seiken*, pp. 112–113, 116, 117, 118.

184 Tazaki, *Abe kantei*, p. 232.

185 Tazaki, *Abe kantei*, p. 232.

186 Tazaki Shirō, 'JA Zenchū', http://gendai.ismedia.jp/articles/-/42013.

187 Mikuriya, *Abe seiken*, p. 111. See below for other, similar terms used to describe the dominance of the Abe-led executive in political and policy affairs.

188 Iinuma, Yoshisuke, 'Abe's New Conservatism: Flood of New Diet Members Decimates LDP "Old Guard"', *The Oriental Economist Report*, Vol. 84, No. 3, March 2016, p. 11.

189 'Anpo "gōin ni oshikiri", Gekkanshi intabyū de Koizumi moto shushō' ['Security Legislation Was "railroaded", Former Prime Minister Koizumi Says in Interview with Monthly Magazine'], *Asahi Shinbun Digital*, 10 December 2015, http://digital.asahi.com/articles/DA3S12109990.html.
190 Mikuriya, *Abe seiken*, p. 106.
191 Mikuriya, *Abe seiken*, p. 113.
192 This is Abe's ideological agenda, including his 'system of principles that consists of "historical understanding", "visiting the Yasukuni Shrine" and exercising the "right of collective self-defence".' Mikuriya, *Abe seiken*, p. 88.
193 Mikuriya, *Abe seiken*, p. 118.
194 Mikuriya, *Abe seiken*, p. 111.
195 Mikuriya, *Abe seiken*, p. 111.
196 His faction also supported the option of abolishing all restrictions on the length of the LDP president's term in office. See also below.
197 Mikuriya, *Abe seiken*, p. 111.
198 Mikuriya, *Abe seiken*, pp. 35–36.
199 Tazaki, *Abe kantei*, p. 231.
200 Takayasu, 'The Pressures of Change', www.nippon.com/en/features/c00410/.
201 Iida, *JA kaitai*, p. 139;
202 Mikuriya, *Abe seiken*, p. 42.
203 Nogami, Tadaoki, '"Shunki kiki" setsu, fujō – Saga shokku no seiken ni -' ['"Spring Crisis" Theory Surfaces – As Administration Deals with the Saga Shock -'], *Nōsei Undō Jānaru*, No. 119, February 2015, p. 8. The reference to the 'ruling parties' is to both the LDP and the Kōmeitō, viz., the ruling coalition parties.
204 'Jimintō – Shuyō yakuin, habatsu baransu jūshi, "Kantei shudō" iji ni fushin' ['LDP – Factional Balance Emphasised in Appointment of Main Party Executives, Efforts Made to Maintain "Kantei Leadership"'], *Mainichi Shinbun*, 4 August 2016, p. 5.
205 Katz, Rick, 'So Strong and Yet So Weak: Abe's Approval: A Mile Wide, Just an Inch Deep', *The Oriental Economist Report*, Vol. 84, No. 3, March 2016, p. 1. See also below.
206 See also Masuyama and Nyblade, 'Japan: The Prime Minister', p. 254.
207 See also Masuyama and Nyblade, 'Japan: The Prime Minister', especially p. 256.
208 Uchiyama, 'Nihon seiji no akutā', p. 14.
209 Uchiyama, 'Nihon seiji no akutā', p. 14. Mori makes the same points arguing that the Japanese prime minister has two major sources of political capital: institutional ('the prime minister's institutional authority over the ruling party and the bureaucracy') and political ('general public support'). See Mori, Satoru, 'Political Leadership in Japan and Japanese Foreign Policy: Lessons from the DPJ Governments', in Sahashi and Gannon (eds), *Looking for Leadership*, pp. 164–165.
210 Uchiyama, 'Nihon seiji no akutā', p. 14.
211 '[Kataru] 15 nen seiji tenbō Anpo hōsei Ji Kō no sa wa umaru Kōmura Masahiko shi' ['[Talk] Political Landscape in 2015, The Gap over Security Legislation between LDP and Kōmeitō Can Be Closed, Kōmura Masahiko'], *Yomiuri Shinbun*, 13 February 2015, p. 4.
212 Miura, Ruri, 'Nōkyō kaikaku no tsugi ni kuru mono' ['What Will Come after JA Reform'], *Miura Ruri* blog, 11 February 2015, http://lullymiura.hatenadiary.jp/entry/2015/02/11/212157.
213 *NHK News 7*, 27 October 2016.
214 *NHK News 7*, 6 March 2017.

215 See also below.
216 'Shushō, jizen no jūryōkyū kiyō, Jimin kanjichō ni Nikai shi', p. 4.
217 'Shushō, jizen no jūryōkyū kiyō, Jimin kanjichō ni Nikai shi', p. 4.
218 'Shushō, jizen no jūryōkyū kiyō, Jimin kanjichō ni Nikai shi', p. 4.
219 'Kantei no sekkyoku zaisei rosen ni kasei Nikai shi, hatafuriyaku ni' ['Nikai Appointed as a Flag-bearer to Support Kantei's Expansionary Fiscal Policy Line'] *Nihon Keizai Shinbun*, 1 September 2016, p. 3.
220 'Jimintō – Shuyō yakuin', p. 5.
221 'Abe's Decision to Tap Nikai for Important LDP Post Alarms Intraparty Rival Factions', *The Mainichi*, 2 August 2016, http://mainichi.jp/english/articles/20160802/p2a/00m/0na/015000c.
222 'Abe's Power Play/Prime Minister Adept at Handling Personnel Matters of Factions, *Yomiuri Shimbun*, 8 March 2015, http://the-japan-news.com/news/article/0001985893.
223 'Abe's Power Play', http://the-japan-news.com/news/article/0001985893.
224 Tazaki, *Abe kantei*, p. 231.
225 Mikuriya, *Abe Seiken*, pp. 37, 125.
226 See also below.
227 Tazaki, *Abe kantei*, p. 231.
228 Takenaka, *Shushō seiji*, p. 157.
229 For example, in his August 2016 reshuffle of LDP executive appointments, Abe was careful to distribute key posts evenly across the factions.
230 A good example is the selection of Shimomura Hakubun, who is close to Abe, as Minister of Education, then as 'special adviser' to the LDP president and then as executive acting secretary-general.
231 'Dai 3 ji saikaizō naikaku Saninsen "shinshō hitsubatsu" iro koku' ['Second Reshuffled Third Abe Cabinet Strongly Reflects "Punishments and Rewards" for Upper House Election'], *Sankei Shinbun* (Osaka HQ edition), 4 August 2016, pp. 1, 3, www.sankei.com/politics/news/160804/plt1608040007-n1.html.
232 See also below.
233 This is the largest faction in the LDP. Machimura died on 1 June 2015.
234 Abe Shinzō o kangaeru kai, *Abe Shinzō to wa nanimono ka?*, p. 84.
235 'Abe's Power Play', http://the-japan-news.com/news/article/0001985893
236 Mikuriya, *Abe seiken*, p. 71.
237 As noted earlier, Amari resigned from his ministerial positions in January 2016 and left Abe's 'inner circle'. He led a small cross-factional group but moved to join the Asō faction in early 2017.
238 'Abe's Power Play', http://the-japan-news.com/news/article/0001985893.
239 Kishida has been quoted as saying, 'Our faction's goal is to realise someday a well-balanced government where Kōchikai holds the reins.' '"Itsuka seiken o" Kishida shi ga iyoku' ['Kishida Indicates Desire to "One Day Take the Reins of Government"'], *Tokyo Shimbun*, 7 September 2016, p. 6.
240 'Abe's Power Play', http://the-japan-news.com/news/article/0001985893.
241 'Abe's Power Play', http://the-japan-news.com/news/article/0001985893.
242 'Abe's Power Play', http://the-japan-news.com/news/article/0001985893.
243 Tazaki, *Abe kantei*, p. 77.
244 Tazaki, *Abe kantei*, p. 77.
245 Abe Shinzō o kangaeru kai, *Abe Shinzō to wa nanimono ka?*, p. 89.
246 Mikuriya, *Abe seiken*, p. 46.

247 Mikuriya, *Abe seiken*, p. 47.
248 'Kenshō manatsu no jinji (jō)', p. 4.
249 Mikuriya, *Abe seiken*, p. 47.
250 Mikuriya, *Abe seiken*, p. 47.
251 'Jimintō – shuyō yakuin', p. 5.
252 Mikuriya, *Abe seiken*, p. 47.
253 Mikuriya, *Abe seiken*, p. 47.
254 Tazaki, *Abe kantei*, p. 78.
255 'Kenshō manatsu no jinji (jō)', p. 4.
256 Yamashita, Kazuhito, 'TPP hantairon wa ronri hatan shite iru' ['The Anti-TPP Logic Is Full of Holes'], *Webronza*, 21 October 2016, http://webronza.asahi.com/business/articles/2016102000003.html.
257 'Shushō no "otomodachi" Yamamoto Yūji Nōsuishō, Ishiba ha de wa uragirimono no yuda' ['Prime Minister's "Friend", MAFF Minister Yūji Yamamoto, Yamamoto Is the Ishiba Faction's Judas'], *Nikkan Gendai*, 15 August 2016, www.nikkan-gendai.com/articles/view/news/187792.
258 'Shushō no "otomodachi"', www.nikkan-gendai.com/articles/view/news/187792.
259 Mikuriya, *Abe seiken*, pp. 50–51.
260 'Nōsei kaikaku, naru ka Shinjirō ryū, Teikō seiryoku ni kirikomu (Shinsō shinsō)' ['Will Shinjirō's Agricultural Policy Reform Produce Results? Cutting into the Resistance Force (Depths of Truth)'], *Nihon Keizai Shinbun*, 3 February 2016, p. 2.
261 See also below.
262 'Ano iwakutsuki no giin', http://president.jp/articles/-/15367.
263 'Ano iwakutsuki no giin', http://president.jp/articles/-/15367.
264 'Ano iwakutsuki no giin', http://president.jp/articles/-/15367.
265 'Nishikawa moto Nōsuishō TPP "uchimaku bon" no zenbun nyūshu, "Abe shushō 'Zoku o motte zoku o seisu'"' ['Full Text of Former MAFF Minister Nishikawa's "Book on the Inside Story" of the TPP Obtained, "Prime Minister Abe Said "Fight Tribe Diet Members with Tribe Diet Members""'], *dot.*, 20 April 2016, http://dot.asahi.com/wa/2016041900209.html.
266 'Nishikawa moto Nōsuishō TPP "uchimaku bon" no zenbun nyūshu', http://dot.asahi.com/wa/2016041900209.html.
267 'Nishikawa moto Nōsuishō TPP "uchimaku bon" no zenbun nyūshu', http://dot.asahi.com/wa/2016041900209.html.
268 Aihara, Ryō, Myōraku, Asako, Oyamada, Kenji and Sumikawa, Takuya (eds), 'Nōkyō kaikaku', http://digital.asahi.com/articles/ASH1N3V8VH1NUTFK00H.html.
269 Aihara, Ryō, Myōraku, Asako, Oyamada, Kenji and Sumikawa, Takuya (eds), 'Nōkyō kaikaku', http://digital.asahi.com/articles/ASH1N3V8VH1NUTFK00H.html.
270 Iida, *JA kaitai*, p. 87.
271 Iida, *JA kaitai*, p. 93.
272 Iida, *JA kaitai*, p. 116.
273 Iida, *JA kaitai*, p. 116.
274 'Koizumi Shinjirō shi, mata nanyaku, Nōgyō ni tsuzuki shakai hoshō kirikomi, Kōrō zoku "giron suru dake"' ['Shinjirō Koizumi Given Another Tough Job to Delve into Social Security Following Agriculture, Health, Labour and Welfare Tribe Diet Members Say "It Will Be All Talk"'], *Sankei Shinbun*, 4 February 2016, p. 5.

275 'Kokunai jinji jōhō' ['Information on Domestic Personnel Affairs'], *Sentaku*, May 2016, p. 11.
276 Ogawa, 'Koizumi Shinjirō Jimin nōrin bukaichō "hitoyose panda" o sotsugyō?', www.sankei.com/premium/news/161202/prm1612020007-n1.html.
277 'Jimin, seisaku kettei ni "ihen", Yosan, zeisei de tetsuzuki kanryakuka aitsugu' ['"Anomaly" in LDP's Policymaking, Procedure Simplified in Relation to Budget and Taxation'], *Nihon Keizai Shinbun* (electronic edition), 30 August 2013, www.nikkei.com/article/DGXNASFS29029_Z20C13A8PP8000/. See also below.
278 Kingston, Jeff, 'Abe's Faltering Efforts to Restart Japan', *Current History*, September 2016, pp. 233–239. See also George Mulgan, Aurelia, 'Media Muzzling under the Abe Administration', in Jeff Kingston (ed.), *Press Freedom in Contemporary Japan*, London and New York, Routledge, 2017, pp. 17–29.
279 Iida, *JA kaitai*, p. 87.
280 'Nōsui fukudaijin, seimukan, keisanzoku zurari, Kaikaku jinarashi? Hirogaru hamon' ['METI Tribe Diet Members Fill MAFF State Minister and Parliamentary Vice-Minister Posts, Is It Groundwork for Reform? Appointment Causes Stir'], *Nihon Keizai Shinbun*, 6 August 2016, p. 4.
281 Iida, *JA kaitai*, p. 87.
282 See also below.
283 Kaihara, Hiroshi, 'The Advent of a New Japanese Politics: Effects of the 1994 Revision of the Electoral Law', *Asian Survey*, Vol. 47, No. 5, 2007, p. 750.
284 Kaihara, 'The Advent of a New Japanese Politics', p. 747.
285 Uchiyama, 'Nihon seiji no akutā', p. 14.
286 Uchiyama, 'Nihon seiji no akutā', p. 14.
287 Prime Minister Mori, for example, appeared to take little interest in the institutions at his disposal. Report Memorandum #01–02, *Central Government Reform in Japan*, www.nsf.gov/od/oise/tokyo/reports/trm/rm01-02.html
288 See also Gaunder, Alisa, *Political Reform in Japan: Leadership Looming Large*, Abingdon and New York, Routledge, 2007. She argues, for example, that 'leadership matters. . . . Leadership is the difference between the successful and unsuccessful cases of reform. . . . A leader with a certain set of resources and personal attributes is . . . needed to persuade self-interested politicians to support reform and then mobilize this support.' (pp. 2, 3).
289 Uchiyama, 'Nihon seiji no akutā', p. 13. Maclachlan also emphasises

> how institutions provide space for the exercise of innovative leadership, and how innovative leaders both adapt to institutions and shape their trajectories. New policymaking and electoral institutions introduced during the 1990s, well before Koizumi assumed power, combined with Koizumi's unique leadership skills, strengthened the prime minister's influence relative to that of the bureaucracy and anti-reformist LDP politicians.

> *Explaining Postal Reform in Japan*, Monday, 11 June 2012, Center for East Asian Studies, University of Texas at Austin, https://liberalarts.utexas.edu/eastasia/news/article.php?id=5495.

290 Tazaki, *Abe kantei*, p. 222.
291 Mikuriya, *Abe seiken*, p. 93.
292 'Shushō Kantei no media kōryaku jutsu' ['The Kantei's Media Strategy'], *Shūkan Tōyō Keizai*, 12 December 2015, pp. 48–51.

293 Mikuriya, *Abe seiken*, p. 67; George Mulgan, 'Media Muzzling under the Abe Administration', forthcoming, 2017.

294 Tazaki, *Abe kantei*, p. 86

295 See the contributions to Kingston (ed.), *Press Freedom*, forthcoming.

296 Abe Shinzō o kangaeru kai, *Abe Shinzō to wa nanimono ka?*, p. 98.

297 Abe Shinzō o kangaeru kai, *Abe Shinzō to wa nanimono ka?*, p. 127.

298 'Seiji jōhō kapuseru' ['Politics: Information Capsule'], *Sentaku*, July 2016, p. 45.

299 Tazaki, *Abe kantei*, p. 89.

300 Kingston, 'Abe's Faltering Efforts to Restart Japan', p. 237.

301 Mikuriya, *Abe seiken*, p. 68.

302 Mikuriya, *Abe seiken*, p. 108.

303 Iinuma, 'Abe's New Conservatism', p. 11. This is the viewpoint advanced in the Rebuild Japan Initiative Foundation's report entitled 'Is Postwar Conservatism Over?'

304 Iinuma, 'Abe's New Conservatism', p. 12, quoting Professor Shimazono Susumu from Tokyo University.

305 Woodall, *Growing Democracy*, p. 25.

306 Woodall, *Growing Democracy*, p. 151.

307 See also Curtis, *Institutional* Change, p. 13, who writes, 'In Japan, the cabinet has traditionally been a body of collective leadership rather than one committed to carrying out the prime minister's program.'

308 Mikuriya *Abe seiken*, p. 32.

309 Curtis, *Japan Update Speech*, p. 6.

310 'Shushō tōben, tsuyoki no wake, Yatō tsuikyū mae ni sente' ['The Reason Behind Prime Minister Abe's Confidence in Responding to Questions in the Diet, He Forestalls the Opposition Parties Before They Start Questioning'], *Nihon Keizai Shinbun*, 28 January 2017, www.nikkei.com/article/DGXLASFS27H56_X20C17A1PP8000/

311 Katō, 'Political Reform', www.tokyofoundation.org/en/articles/2008/political-reform-of-the-japanese-system-of-government-symposium-report-2.

312 Katō, 'Political Reform', www.tokyofoundation.org/en/articles/2008/political-reform-of-the-japanese-system-of-government-symposium-report-2.

313 Curtis wrote, 'Many cabinet ministers have seen their job as representing the interests of their ministry, meaning interests as defined by ministry bureaucrats, rather than imposing the demands of the prime minister on the bureaucrats under their charge.' *Institutional Change*, p. 13.

314 Hanatani, '"Kantei ikkyō"', p. 25.

315 The ministers in charge (of certain issues) are posts for dealing with short-term policies that are considered to be important at the time. In contrast, the ministers of state for special missions are designed to deal with longer-term issues.

316 Mikuriya, *Abe seiken*, p. 129.

317 Mikuriya, *Abe seiken*, pp. 107, 108.

318 Iio, *Nihon no tōchi kōzō*, pp. 82, 83.

319 'Jimin, seisaku kettei ni "ihen"', www.nikkei.com/article/DGXNASFS29029_Z20C13A8PP8000/.

320 'Jimin, seisaku kettei ni "ihen"', www.nikkei.com/article/DGXNASFS29029_Z20C13A8PP8000/.

321 Tazaki, *Abe kantei*, p. 219.

322 George Mulgan, Aurelia, 'Securitizing the TPP in Japan: Policymaking Structure and Discourse', *Asia Policy*, 22, July 2016, p. 197.

323 'Anpo "gōin ni oshikiri"', http://ajw.asahi.com/article/behind_news/politics/AJ201512100057.
324 "Anpo "gōin ni oshikiri"', http://ajw.asahi.com/article/behind_news/politics/AJ201512100057.
325 George Mulgan, 'Loosening the Ties That Bind', pp. 221–246.
326 'Amari shi, tō sōmu ni shūnin, Yatō wa nao sekinin tsuikyū' ['Amari to Serve on LDP Executive Council, Opposition Parties Continue to Pursue His Responsibility'], *Nihon Keizai Shinbun*, 30 August 2016, p. 3.
327 'Nōkyō kaikaku', www.nikkei.com/article/DGXLASFS09H7E_Z00C15A2EA2000/.
328 Miura, 'Nōkyō kaikaku', http://lullymiura.hatenadiary.jp/entry/2015/02/11/212157.
329 Nogami, '"Shunki kiki" setsu', p. 9.
330 *Abe seiken*, pp. 128–129.
331 This process was called *gosetsumei* (explanation) and it involved the bureaucrats explaining their planned policies and legislation to LDP Diet members. See Iio, *Nihon no tōchi kōzō*, p. 53.
332 Iio, *Nihon no tōchi kōzō*, p. 103.
333 George Mulgan, 'Loosening the Ties That Bind', pp. 221–246.
334 Hanatani, '"Kantei ikkyō"', p. 25.
335 George Mulgan, 'Loosening the Ties That Bind', pp. 221–246.
336 'Jimin, seisaku kettei ni "ihen"', www.nikkei.com/article/DGXNASFS29029_Z20C13A8PP8000/.
337 'Jimin, seisaku kettei ni "ihen"', www.nikkei.com/article/DGXNASFS29029_Z20C13A8PP8000/.
338 Iio, *Nihon no tōchi kōzō*, p. 83.
339 'Oshikomareta Jimin zeichō, Shushō gawa kōsei, taichō ichidan to' ['LDP Tax Research Commission Pushed Back, Prime Minister's Side Takes the Offensive, LDP Retreats Further'], *Nihon Keizai Shinbun*, 31 December 2014, www.nikkei.com/article/DGXLASFS30H5L_Q4A231C1EA1000/.
340 'Jimin, seisaku kettei ni "ihen"', www.nikkei.com/article/DGXNASFS29029_Z20C13A8PP8000/.
341 'Jimin, seisaku kettei ni "ihen"', www.nikkei.com/article/DGXNASFS29029_Z20C13A8PP8000/.
342 'Oshikomareta Jimin zeichō', www.nikkei.com/article/DGXLASFS30H5L_Q4A231C1EA1000/.
343 'Oshikomareta Jimin zeichō', www.nikkei.com/article/DGXLASFS30H5L_Q4A231C1EA1000/.
344 'Oshikomareta Jimin zeichō', www.nikkei.com/article/DGXLASFS30H5L_Q4A231C1EA1000/.
345 'Oshikomareta Jimin zeichō', www.nikkei.com/article/DGXLASFS30H5L_Q4A231C1EA1000/.
346 'Oshikomareta Jimin zeichō', www.nikkei.com/article/DGXLASFS30H5L_Q4A231C1EA1000/.
347 'Oshikomareta Jimin zeichō', www.nikkei.com/article/DGXLASFS30H5L_Q4A231C1EA1000/.
348 'Oshikomareta Jimin zeichō', www.nikkei.com/article/DGXLASFS30H5L_Q4A231C1EA1000/.
349 'Oshikomareta Jimin zeichō', www.nikkei.com/article/DGXLASFS30H5L_Q4A231C1EA1000/.

350 'Oshikomareta Jimin zeichō', www.nikkei.com/article/DGXLASFS30H5L_Q4A231C1EA1000/.
351 'Zeichō innā ni Amari shi ga kanyū e' ['Amari to Join "Inner Circle" of LDP Tax Commission'], *Yomiuri Shinbun*, 24 September 2016, p. 4.
352 As Mikuriya points out, 'Before the decline of the LDP started, the [balance of power] always swung back [to the party], so the Kantei and the party always ended up working closely together.' *Abe seiken*, p. 129.
353 Makihara, 'Seisaku kettei ni okeru shushō Kantei no yakuwari', www.nippon.com/ja/features/c00408/.

4 Westminster or presidential?

Given the concentration of power in the Abe prime ministerial executive, the question arises whether Japan is transitioning either to a more Westminster-style system or to a more presidential-style system. Both models appear to be relevant given that Westminster systems are characterised by a 'strong executive'[1] and in presidential systems, power is personalised in a single political leader.[2]

Japan's 'un-Westminster' path

In terms of the structural evolution of Japan's political system, several developments associated with the rise of the prime ministerial executive suggest that Japan is moving towards a more Westminster style of government. The central features of Westminster systems are strong cabinet government and the fusion of executive and legislative authority.[3] The prime minister chooses the cabinet, the cabinet under the prime minister decides government policy, and the parliamentary party supports government policy and passes it into legislation. The line of policymaking authority is top-down: prime ministers normally carry their cabinets, cabinets normally carry the parliamentary party and the parliamentary party normally carries the parliament.[4] The parliamentary party is subordinate to the formal political executive and does not function as an alternative locus of policymaking. Similarly, the bureaucracy supports the cabinet, follows ministers' instructions and implements policy as agreed by the cabinet.[5]

The question is whether the evolutionary shifts now occurring in Japan's political system are taking it further towards this Westminster model of parliamentary-cabinet government. The traditional constraints on the policymaking powers of the prime minister and cabinet – the party and the bureaucracy – which were the primary obstacles to Japan's transition to a Westminster system in earlier years – are much diminished in stature and power. The relative decline in the influence of the bureaucracy means that ministers are now more dominant over their ministries and the cabinet is collectively stronger vis-à-vis the bureaucracy. The ruling party is now more centralised under its executive leadership and the prime minister and the cabinet's hands are no longer necessarily tied by the party's policy demands, given the prime ministerial executive's failure always to observe the convention of prior approval by the LDP. Broadly speaking, policymaking power in Japan's political system has become more centralised and more top-down.

These developments certainly appear to be indicative of a Westminsterising trend. However, countervailing developments suggest an anti-Westminster shift. First, while bureaucrats are less influential relative to their ministers individually and the cabinet collectively, both the bureaucracy *and their ministers* are more subject to the power of the prime ministerial executive. Ministers are still not members of the highest executive authority responsible for determining national policy. The cabinet is very much Prime Minister Abe's cabinet and ministers are clearly subordinate to the prime minister and even Suga. So while bureaucrats may be exercising less influence in terms of initiating and advancing their desired policies and requiring their ministers to speak for these policies, this does not necessarily ensure that the cabinet itself has become the supreme, authoritative source of government policy.

Secondly, the relative decline in the power of the ruling party as an independent policymaking actor, with separate *party interests* in the policymaking process, falls short as a Westminsterising force for two reasons. The first is that the ruling party is still not united under the cabinet and separate ruling party policymaking bodies continue to function. Senior party leaders and policy executives, such as the chairmen of the PARC and Executive Council, are not in the cabinet, which would have united the party with the formal political executive.[6] Nor are politicians banned from coming into contact with bureaucrats.[7] To some extent Japan remains, as the DPJ's manifesto put it in 2009, a 'two-track system in which policy making proceeds in parallel in government and in the ruling party' and has still not reached the stage where it is 'a unitary system of Cabinet-centered policy making.'[8] As in the past, the ruling party (*yotō*) is still not the 'government party' (*seikentō*) because a clear distinction remains between the government (*seifu*) and the ruling party as two quite separate organisations.[9] The situation in Japan thus continues to diverge from the principle of a united government and government party as in other countries that have Westminster-style political systems.[10] A strengthening of the leadership of the prime minister has been achieved without the integration of the ruling party and the government.[11] As Shimizu correctly argues, the reforms that came out of Hashimoto's administrative reform, which reinforced the Kantei's functions, 'did not extend to "political reform" including the relationship between the cabinet and the ruling party.'[12]

The second reason is that declining party policymaking power is not necessarily commensurate with the centralisation of policymaking power in the cabinet. While it has become more difficult for ordinary ruling party members to act against the will of the prime ministerial executive, they are still not subordinate to the cabinet.[13] There may be a greater fusion of legislative and executive power because the LDP is more under the thumb of the executive than it was, but it is the prime ministerial executive not the formal political executive. In other words, policymaking authority has shifted from the party to the prime ministerial executive rather than to the prime minister and cabinet.

Koizumi, for example, may have reclaimed 'real decision-making power from the party "old guard" and the bureaucracy',[14] but this was no guarantee that he moved the decision-making system in a Westminster direction.[15] A Westminster system does not centralise 'power in the hands of the party leadership and prime minister'.[16] It centralises power in the hands of the prime minister and cabinet. In other words, the expansion of prime ministerial authority does not automatically take Japan in a Westminister direction. A stronger and more influential prime minister is a necessary, but not a sufficient, condition for Westminster-style government. The repositioning of power under Koizumi buttressed the prime minister and the Kantei's role in policymaking, but it did not enhance the role of the cabinet as a policymaking body.[17] As the author has argued elsewhere, the fact remains that 'strengthening the prime minister does not automatically strengthen the ministers. . . . [P]arliamentary cabinet systems are systems of collective leadership rather than personal leadership'.[18] An expanded role for the prime minister *in the cabinet* alongside an equally expanded and more influential role for the other ministers – as a *collective* policymaking group – is a crucial requirement for Westminster government. Koizumi buttressed the power of the prime ministerial executive *independently of the cabinet*, which remained on the sidelines of the real policymaking power structures.[19] Moreover, under Abe, it has become even more abundantly clear that the balance of policymaking power has shifted further in favour of the prime ministerial executive – against the bureaucracy, against the ruling party and even against his own cabinet ministers. The legislative agenda is set by the Kantei, which has usurped the role of the cabinet in deciding the general course of government policy.[20]

Thirdly, while policymaking is now distinctly more centralised and more top-down, centralised top-down leadership under the prime minister or the prime ministerial executive does not equate to Westminister-style leadership. This misconception is evident in the analysis of security policymaking under the Koizumi administration.[21] As already noted, it is the prime minister and cabinet as a collective decision-making body that exercises centralised, top-down policy leadership in Westminster systems. The increasing centralisation of policymaking authority in the prime ministerial executive is creating prime ministerial executive government, not cabinet government. The path towards invigorated executive leadership has taken the form of stronger and more activist *prime ministers and their executive*, not stronger and more activist prime ministers and their cabinets.

Moreover, the rise of the prime ministerial executive in Japan is not a narrative about the rise of Japanese prime ministers as policy leaders. It is a narrative about the rise of prime minister *and* those institutions supporting his executive leadership on policy issues. As argued in this book, this development has been primarily due to the process of central government reform, giving the prime ministerial executive new roles and functions in policymaking and expanding its influence *relative to the cabinet and its ministers*, the ruling party and the bureaucracy, and thus effectively adding a new and powerful executive layer of government to which all other rival power centres are subordinate. The high point of this trend has been reached under Prime Minister Abe. Although his political power base is in the ruling party in the parliament, and although the cabinet has a stable parliamentary base in both houses of the Diet,[22] Abe's executive power base is in the Kantei and its support structures, rather than in the cabinet or the parliament. This explains the 'puzzle' of why a more powerful prime ministerial executive in Japan has not produced a Westminster-style system. Japan still does not have cabinet government where the prime minister and cabinet are the supreme authoritative decision-making body.

Japan has thus responded in an 'un-Westminster' fashion to the need for stronger and more effective political leadership. The centralisation of power that has occurred in the Japanese political system has primarily affected the prime minister, the Kantei and executive support structures, not the prime minister and cabinet. In fact, the invigorated power of the prime ministerial executive, particularly under Abe, has taken Japan even further away from the Westminster model by undermining the cabinet and its ministers, which have become, both individually and collectively, more subservient to the prime minister and his executive. In this way, the Abe prime ministerial executive has displaced the cabinet as the core policymaking authority. Japan has 'effective executive leadership'[23] but not cabinet government. The fact thus remains that 'cabinet government has failed to take root in Japan'.[24] As Woodall correctly concludes, 'Japan has failed to institutionalize cabinet government. . . . The cabinet has never become the foremost executive organ, as expected in a Westminster system'.[25]

Although Westminster systems are periodically under challenge from strong prime ministers, particularly in the United Kingdom where there have been examples of strong prime ministers sidelining cabinets in decision-making,[26] in terms of well-entrenched political conventions and norms, the Westminister traditions of strong cabinet government remain solid in such polities and they tend to revert to a more Westminster style of government under different prime ministers, depending on their personal political style. Moreover, the model of Westminster government as strong cabinet government is one to which countries can aspire or approximate to greater or lesser degrees. This is an empirical question that needs to be answered in each case, with answers varying according to different countries at different times. While even the UK may stray from the Westminster model from time to time, the basic model remains unchanged. Even if some argue that Westminster systems have become more 'presidentialised' under particular prime ministers and matching developments have taken place in Japan with more formidable prime ministerial leaders such as Nakasone, Koizumi and Abe, 'presidential-style' prime ministers in parliamentary systems are best seen as a variation within the Westminster system of cabinet government rather than as a remodelling of it.

Moreover, although the intention of Japan's administrative reformers was to strengthen the prime minister *and the cabinet*, in practice, this process succeeded in expanding the policymaking power of the prime minister and his executive rather than the prime minister and his cabinet. Japan is not becoming more Westminster. If anything, as some have argued, it is becoming more 'presidential'. However, 'presidentialising' the prime ministership is also an 'un-Westminster path' and whether prime ministers such as Nakasone, Koizumi and Abe can be accurately described as 'presidential' remains very much a subject of debate.

A more 'presidential' prime minister?

A number of scholars have referred to Japan's 'presidential prime ministers' (*daitōryōteki shushō*),[27] meaning those who have 'started to acquire presidential-like characteristics',[28] and to the 'presidentialisation of the parliamentary cabinet system' (*giin naikakusei no daitōryōsei ka*).[29] Pempel even argued that administrative reform presidentialised the Japanese prime ministership by giving the prime minister 'explicit authority to engage in policy planning and to initiate legislation',[30] by allocating drafting and coordination functions to a bolstered Cabinet Secretariat and by establishing the new, large Cabinet Office.[31] The Cabinet Office itself could be considered as 'roughly equivalent to the Executive Office of the President (EoP) in the United States, an organization created in 1939 with the explicit purpose of helping the President of the United States . . . control his own government.'[32]

Amongst Japanese prime ministers highly motivated by strong policy convictions and anxious to develop and exploit the prime minister's formal power resources, Nakasone and Koizumi stand out as more presidential than others in both leadership style and *modus operandi*. Nakasone, for example, had his own strong, personal policy agenda and a burning ambition to see it implemented, searching for ways around the traditional policymaking process in order to do so. He also used his own personal popularity with the Japanese public to boost his policymaking authority, including skilful use of the media to push various policy objectives. In addition, he employed personal and official advisory groups to develop public and political support for his policy preferences and as an aide to neutralise opposition from within the bureaucracy and ruling party.[33] These were all tactics that helped to support what has been described as a top-down, presidential style of leadership.[34] As Shinoda observes, Nakasone wanted to 'exercise stronger political leadership as a "president-like" prime minister'.[35]

Likewise, Koizumi's response to the obstacles he faced when his policy initiatives were blunted by the bureaucracy and vested interests in the LDP was 'to try to turn the Japanese system into a top-down system by presidentializing the prime ministership.'[36] As Woodall remarks, 'Koizumi's "presidential" leadership style led to speculation that prime ministerial government might become the rule'.[37] Certainly, many in the ruling party during his administration objected to his so-called 'presidential system-style techniques'.[38] As Mikuriya argues, 'Koizumi wanted to do everything that a prime minister could do and aspired to achieve a presidential system.'[39] Koizumi certainly presented a very high personal profile in election campaigns, emphasised direct relations with the mass media and the voting public over relations with his majority party in the parliament, and extensively relied on personally appointed staff such as Takenaka over bureaucrats in developing policies that he wanted to implement.[40] Some even accused him of being a 'dictator' on issues such as privatising the postal service and the Japan Public Highway Corporation and, in the diplomatic field, engineering a breakthrough visit to North Korea in 2002 and proactively supporting the United States in Iraq in 2003.

On the other hand, for other matters, as Tazaki points out, 'Koizumi literally left the decision-making to others such as then-Chief Cabinet Secretary Fukuda Yasuo and various cabinet members'.[41] His administration

> functioned on the basis of . . . Koizumi's strong ability to send messages. Koizumi's comments were mocked as 'one-phrase politics', but his ability to leave an impression on people's minds was unrivalled by any other prime minister. . . . Using the power of his words, Koizumi kept the LDP and opposition parties in check and appealed to the people. . . . However, the administration's decision-making system itself was orthodox. Koizumi used executive secretaries to the prime minister . . . listened to the various ministries' views, and entrusted [the ministries] with most matters.[42]

In other words, generalising about the nature of policymaking in the Koizumi administration from specific examples where Koizumi conducted himself in a 'president-like' fashion and demonstrated 'president-like' powers does not provide the full picture. When, for example, in December 2004, Koizumi met with first-term Lower House members from the LDP, he said, 'It is important to strike a balance between dictating and leaving decisions to others.'[43] In other words, he 'distinguished between policies that he himself decided and carried out, and policies that he delegated to members of his cabinet.'[44]

Prime Minister Abe has also been described as having 'president-like' qualities. As Mikuriya posits, 'Abe's mindset as prime minister is much stronger than his mindset as LDP leader. He thinks of himself as leading the nation overall, not just a political party. In other words, he has a presidential mindset [*daitōryōteki ishiki*].'[45] Moreover, like Koizumi, Abe selects cabinet members and others without reference to the party, is even more dominant as the leader of his party and has a high profile in election campaigns.

On the other hand, in contrast to Koizumi, Abe does not seek to go over the heads of the LDP's Diet members and 'appeal directly to the electorate and earn the confidence [of the people]'.[46] There has been no pronounced 'shift from more collective partified forms of politics to personalized ones in terms of executive, party and electoral process (sic.) respectively.'[47] In this respect, Koizumi's prime ministership was more presidentialised than Abe's given Koizumi's desire for presidential powers in order to overcome what he saw were formidable obstacles to his policy initiatives in the policymaking process. Abe is different: even on the issue of constitutional reform, which reflects his deeply held ideological convictions, he appreciates the importance of taking his party, the coalition and as many Diet members as possible with him. Hence, on politically difficult issues, particularly involving the broader electorate or entrenched lobbies such as agriculture, he is prepared to negotiate outcomes and make well-timed concessions, if necessary, in order to achieve his larger goal. His policy agenda is advanced in a fashion designed not to arouse strong opposition from any quarter and thus moves forward in a way that offers a greater chance of successful implementatioin. In short, Abe can be cautious and a conciliator rather than acting in a uniformly dictatorial or presidential manner. Despite his dominance over his ministers and within cabinet, his prime ministerial leadership style is still closer to the 'chairman of the board' model rather than the 'presidential' model.[48] He is the 'primus inter pares of a collective "inner core", or "inner circle"'[49] – namely the prime ministerial executive.

In another contrast to Koizumi, 'Abe's ability to send messages is not as strong'.[50] He may be the leading personality in the government from a media perspective and he may also be the primary focus of public opinion in terms of gaining public support for his administration's policies. However, he remains an important but not the sole focus of media interest in his government and his public face is that of the leader of his party as a fairly united force. In this respect, Abe still governs *through* his party. He may be the principal face of the LDP in elections, but he does not separate himself from it in terms of his policy positions as Koizumi did in 2005. In this respect, unlike Koizumi, Abe has not personalised the electoral process.[51] Although strongly shaped by his own political agenda, Abe's policies are still the party's policies. He has strong control over the party while not being independent of it. He prefers to carry the party with him rather than operating as 'an autonomous political force'.[52]

Moreover, given the strength of other political figures in Abe's administration, such as Suga, and the patent institutional powers of the prime ministerial executive as a collection of supporting policy actors, it is clear that Abe operates within a collective rather than an individual leadership framework. Power does not reside in just the prime minister even within the executive itself. It is shared amongst a group of actors in the Kantei, each with their own resources and operating with 'complex interdependencies'.[53] Abe's executive power base is thus institutional, not individual, and his control over the government is less individualistic and presidential than collective and broadly based. In his administration, it is clear that executive power does not reside in a single individual as in a presidential system.[54] Certainly he does not exercise personalised power to the degree that it 'marks a shift from a collective to a more individualised form of executive government.'[55] Nor is it his ambition to be a presidential leader: he prefers to enlist key individuals and groups within the prime ministerial executive to support his prime ministership. Power has become more centralised in the Kantei under the Abe prime ministership, with individual ministers and the cabinet acting more as agents of the prime ministerial executive but, at the same time, policymaking still requires processes of complex coordination involving a range of players, the party and the bureaucracy included, despite the relative decline in their policymaking powers. There are, therefore, many processes of collective decision-making and complex interdependencies at play.

Thus, on balance, although Koizumi was more 'presidential' than Abe, neither prime minister, for different reasons, 'presidentialised' politics in Japan's parliamentary cabinet system in the sense of altering the regime in a more presidential direction. The degree of personalisation of leadership power and prime ministerial autonomy is insufficient to count as the 'presidentialisation' of the prime ministership. Certainly power is more centralised, but it is centralised in the prime minister and his executive rather than in the prime minister alone. It is, therefore, a system of collective leadership rather than individual leadership. It is patently clear that Abe operates within a collective leadership framework. He does not personally decide the priorities and direction of the government.[56] Nor is there a sufficient level of personalisation of the electoral process in terms of separation from his party and key personnel in his broader administration.[57]

Finally, the emergence of strong prime ministers and the rise of a strong prime ministerial executive in Japan are not necessarily incompatible with a parliamentary cabinet system and do not necessarily signify a broader shift towards a presidential system. The institutions of presidential and parliamentary cabinet systems remain divergent as illustrated, for example, by the contrast between Japan and the United States. Strengthening the powers of the prime minister in Japan has merely emphasised powers associated with that office in a parliamentary cabinet system. As for the personalisation of leadership, it occurs in both parliamentary and presidential systems and does not necessarily make a parliamentary system *more like* a presidential one.[58]

Notes

1 Grube, Dennis C. and Howard, Cosmo, 'Is the Westminster System Broken Beyond Repair?', *Governance*, Vol. 29, No. 4, October 2016, p. 468.
2 As Dowding puts it, talking about the 'presidentialization of the prime minister' is designed to get across the idea that 'government revolves around a single person'. Dowding, Keith, 'The Prime Ministerialisation of the British Prime Minister', *Parliamentary Affairs*, Vol. 13, 2013, p. 617.
3 George Mulgan, Aurelia, 'Japan's "Un-Westminster" System: Impediments to Reform in a Crisis Economy', *Government and Opposition*, Vol. 38, No. 1, January 2003, p. 80. See also Krauss, Ellis S. and Pekkanen, Robert J., *The Rise and Fall of Japan's LDP: Political Party Organizations as Historical Institutions*, Ithaca, NY, Cornell University Press, 2010, p. 259.
4 George Mulgan, 'Japan's "Un-Westminster" System', p. 76.
5 George Mulgan, 'Japan's "Un-Westminster" System', p. 80.
6 As Shimizu points out, in the United Kingdom (UK),

> most of the main ruling party leaders and executives are appointed to government posts such as ministers and junior ministers. . . . It is impossible for someone with influence like a faction leader to stay in the ruling party without occupying a government post and [for them] publicly to make claims that are different to those made the cabinet.

Keizai zaisei senki – Kantei shudō shudō Koizumi kara Abe e [*History of the Economic and Fiscal War – Kantei Leadership, from Koizumi to Abe*], Tokyo, Nihon Keizai Shinbun Shuppansha, 2007, p. 224.
7 As Shimizu argues, in the UK, 'Politicians who are not in public positions are basically banned from coming into contact with bureaucrats. Politicians can only exercise political influence on bureaucrats through government posts such as prime minister, minister and junior minister.' *Kantei shudō*, p. 224.
8 The Democratic Party of Japan, *2009 Change of Government, the Democratic Party of Japan's Platform for Government*, www.dpj.or.jp/english/manifesto/manifesto2009.pdf, p. 4.

9 Iio, Jun, *Nihon no tōchi kōzō*, p. 79. As Iio argues, 'there is something called the Government and Ruling Party Liaison Conference [*seifu yotō renraku kaigi*]. This meeting is held by the government and the ruling party for liaison purposes and is premised on a clear distinction between the two' (p. 78). The Liaison Conference continues to function under the Abe administration.

10 Iio, *Nihon no tōchi kōzō*, p. 79.

11 Shiozaki Yasuhisa, 'Changes in the Japanese Policymaking Process', in Thomas E. Mann and Takeshi Sasaki (eds), *Governance for a New Century: Japanese Challenges, American Experience*, Tokyo, Japan Center for International Exchange, 2002, p. 60.

12 Shimizu, *Kantei shudō*, p. 225.

13 Cf. Machidori's definition of a Westminster system 'where it is difficult for general ruling party members to act against the will of the core executive once the prime minister is selected'. *Shushō seiji*, p. 167.

14 See, for example, Estevez-Abe, Margarita, 'Japan's Shift Toward a Westminster System', *Asian Survey*, Vol. 46, No. 4, p. 650. According to Mishima, however, Koizumi 'largely failed to undercut traditional bureaucratic strength.' 'Grading Japanese Prime Minister Koizumi's Revolution', p. 728. See also George Mulgan, *Japan's Failed Revolution*, pp. 129–212.

15 Estevez-Abe, 'Japan's Shift Toward a Westminster System', p. 651. See also Shinoda Tomohito, 'Japan's Top-Down Policy Process to Dispatch the SDF to Iraq', *Japanese Journal of Political Science*, Vol. 7, No. 1, 2006, pp. 71–91.

16 Estevez-Abe, 'Japan's Shift Toward a Westminster System', p. 633. The party leadership in Japan consists not only of the president, but also the vice-president and secretary-general and arguably those who chair the PARC and Executive Council. Only the president is a member of the cabinet. Moreover, centralising power in the hands of the prime minister does not strengthen the cabinet in itself.

17 Cf. Shinoda, 'Japan's Top-Down Policy Process', pp. 71–91.

18 George Mulgan, 'The Politics of Economic Reform', p. 271.

19 Shimizu maintains, however, that 'the changes made under the Koizumi government ensure the eventual emergence of cabinet government'. Quoted in Woodall, *Growing Democracy*, p. 24, citing Shimizu, *Kantei shudō*, p. 404.

20 Takenaka also emphasises the independent powers of the Diet over parliamentary business, pointing out that

> under the Japanese parliamentary system, the cabinet has no power over parliamentary business and legislative affairs. . . . [T]he ability of the Diet to control its own business and to legislate virtually independently of the cabinet . . . gives the backbenchers significant power to affect legislative agendas and schedules.

Takenaka Harukata, 'The Frequent Turnover of Japanese Prime Ministers: Still a Long Way to a Westminster Model', in Sahashi and Gannon (eds), *Looking for Leadership*, p. 53. In short, Japan lacks another aspect of the fusion of executive and legislative authority characteristic of Westminster systems.

21 Shinoda, 'Japan's Top-Down Policy Process', pp. 71–91. Shinoda also argues that Japan became more Westminster because the executive authority of the Kantei and Cabinet Secretariat as support structures for the prime minister was boosted, but this is not the same as bolstering the authority of the cabinet as a decision-making body and so does not qualify as a 'new style of Westminster system' (p. 71).

22 Masuyama and Nyblade argue that the performance of the executive in terms of its demonstrating leadership qualities depends critically on its 'power base both inside and outside the parliament', namely whether or not 'the cabinet has a stable parliamentary base' and 'whether or not the general public supports the cabinet'. 'Japan: The Prime Minister', p. 250.

23 Woodall, *Growing Democracy*, p. 211.

24 Woodall, *Growing Democracy*, p. 29.

25 Woodall, *Growing Democracy*, p. 212.

26 Connors, 'Next Steps for Japan, p. 112.

27 Sakano, *The Presidentialization of Politics*, p. 1 *et passim*, and Machidori, *Shushō seiji*, p. 67.

28 Machidori, *Shushō seiji*, p. 68.

29 Machidori, *Shushō seiji*, p. 68.

30 Pempel, 'Between Pork and Productivity: The Collapse of the Liberal Democratic Party', *Journal of Japanese Studies*, Vol. 36, No. 2, Summer 2010, p. 244.

31 Pempel, 'Between Pork and Productivity', p. 244.

32 Report Memorandum #01–02, *Central Government Reform in Japan*, www.nsf.gov/od/oise/tokyo/reports/trm/rm01-02.html.

33 Angel, 'Prime Ministerial Leadership in Japan', pp. 591–600.

34 Angel, 'Prime Ministerial Leadership in Japan', p. 601.

35 Shinoda, *Koizumi Diplomacy*, p. 16.

36 George Mulgan, 'The Politics of Economic Reform', p. 271.

37 Woodall, *Growing Democracy*, p. 177.

38 Iio, *Nihon no tōchi kōzō*, p. 200.

39 Mikuriya, *Abe seiken*, p. 179.

40 Machidori writes,

> Some specific characteristics of a presidential prime minister include emphasising direct relations with the mass media and general voters more than their relationship with the majority in the parliament and placing more importance on staff members, who were politically appointed based on personal relationships with the prime minister, than bureaucrats in policy development.

Shushō seiji, p. 71. See also below.

41 Tazaki, *Abe kantei*, p. 39.

42 Tazaki, *Abe kantei*, pp. 38, 39.

43 Tazaki, *Abe kantei*, p. 39.

44 Tazaki, *Abe kantei*, p. 39.

45 Mikuriya, *Abe seiken*, p. 129.

46 Sakano, *The Presidentialization of Politics*, p. 3.

47 Sakano, *The Presidentialization of Politics*, pp. 3–4.

48 A useful contrast between the two models of the prime minister's role – the 'presidential' and 'chairman' models is drawn by Takayasu, Kensuke, in 'The Pressures of Change', www.nippon.com/en/features/c00410/.

49 Professor Brian Woodall, personal communication, 27 October 2016.

50 Tazaki, *Abe kantei*, p. 39.

51 Sakano argues that 'personalization of the electoral process' is one of the definitions of a presidential prime ministership. 'Abstract', *The Presidentialization of Politics*.

52 Mughan, Anthony. *Media and the Presidentialization of Parliamentary Election*, New York, Palgrave, 2000, p. 7.

53 Heffernan, *Presidentialization in the United Kingdom,* p. 12.
54 Takayasu, 'The Pressures of Change', www.nippon.com/en/features/c00410/.
55 Heffernan, *Presidentialization in the United Kingdom,* p. 8.
56 As Takayasu writes, 'the top-down or presidential model envisages that the prime minister will personally decide the priorities and direction of the government, treating cabinet ministers as subordinates, and taking a leadership role by becoming directly involved in the policy-making process.' 'The Pressures of Change', www.nippon.com/en/features/c00410/.
57 Sakano, 'Abstract', *The Presidentialization of Politics.*
58 This discussion owes much to Dowding, 'The Prime Ministerialisation of the British Prime Minister', pp. 617–635.

5 Conclusion

The question of 'who leads?' in Japan is no longer a matter of conjecture. With the advent of the second Abe administration, the answer is clear-cut: 'the prime minister and his executive office', backed up by a substantial policy support apparatus. In being able to exert formidable power and authority over government policy, Abe owes much to a number of his predecessors, particularly Prime Ministers Nakasone, Hashimoto and Koizumi. Each made an important contribution to modernising Japan's political system by advancing the process of administrative reform, which included important changes to central government structures centring on the prime minister. These changes produced the necessary institutional innovations to allow the prime minister to assert policy leadership and culminated in the emergence of the 'prime ministerial executive', a structure of policymaking that has become much more prominent and powerful in Japan in recent years.

The result has been to turn Japan's traditional, decentralised, bottom-up policymaking process on its head and significantly alter power relations between the prime ministerial executive and the principal countervailing centres of power in the bureaucracy and in the ruling LDP. The structural changes to the policymaking system have incontrovertibly altered the distribution of power within the Japanese political system.

The book has attempted to illuminate how the prime ministerial executive is operating under the Abe prime ministership. There is no doubt that, under Abe's guiding hand, a very much stronger Kantei has emerged. In a number of key ways, he has powerfully reinforced the Kantei's position as the executive agency of the Japanese government and of his prime ministership, ensuring that Japan now has a Kantei-centred policymaking system assisted by an upper layer of core government offices focussed on providing the Kantei with wide-ranging policy support. Abe is also drawing on an extraordinarily strong personnel support structure. His astute appointments to various cabinet and party posts include that of Chief Cabinet Secretary Suga who demonstrates formidable power and acumen, particularly with respect to managing the bureaucracy and the cabinet. Politically, the Abe administration has also benefited from its impressive performance in elections and a weakening of rival factional power centres within the LDP, which have traditionally limited prime ministerial powers. Finally, Abe has been able to draw on his own personal resources, including a capacity for setting clear policy directions and for exercising strong political leadership.

The larger question posed by these political developments is what direction the Japanese political system is headed. Is it becoming more Westminster or more presidential? The answer to this question is far from clear-cut as there are elements taking Japan both further towards and away from these models of governance. Perhaps the most important questions are not whether Japan under Prime Minister Abe is moving towards a Westminster or presidential system but whether Abe will succeed in institutionalising the prime ministerial executive and whether this has now reached a stage that could be described as 'the executive domination of government'.[1] Certainly Abe has embarked on a process of buttressing the policy authority of the Japanese prime minister together with that of his executive office and its policy and administrative support apparatus in order to facilitate the exercise of his own individual policy authority in concert with the prime ministerial executive as a whole. He took advantage of precedents and reforms made by predecessors such as Nakasone, Hashimoto and Koizumi and pushed them even further. In this way, he advanced the process of institutionalising executive power in Japan, although whether his successors will succeed in deploying power in the same way as Abe and in entrenching the power of the prime ministerial executive remains to be seen.

The risks presented by the Abe administration also lie in the enhanced authority and domination of the prime ministerial executive in policymaking, almost sweeping all before it. Given that Japan's traditional policymaking model has been largely overturned, there are fewer institutional checks and balances on a strong prime ministerial executive, with a more subordinate bureaucracy, a more subservient cabinet and a weakened ruling party. It is now difficult to identify where the political checks and balances are, given the LDP's strong majorities in both houses of the Diet, together with the Abe administration's media 'manipulation' and high-handed management of Diet debates. Evidence of these trends includes Abe's attempts to subdue media and opposition criticism, which are encouraged by the relative weakness of anti-Abe factions in his own party and by the largely ineffective performance of the opposition parties in the Diet. So, while delivering a stable political cycle, the Abe administration remains largely unchecked – by institutional, organisational or political mechanisms.[2]

Added to this are Abe's own authoritarian proclivities, which are reflected in the LDP's proposals for constitutional change and in Abe's personal demonstrations of a poor understanding of and respect for the fundamental principles of democratic accountability. How these trends will play out over what may turn out to be an extended term in office for the prime minister remains to be seen. When combined with the changing nature of Japanese political institutions bestowing immense power and policymaking authority on the prime ministerial executive, it raises questions about the future of Japanese democracy itself.

Notes

1 Maki, John M., 'Executive Power in Japan', *Far Eastern Survey*, Vol. 24, No. 5, May 1955, p. 75.
2 Curtis first highlighted this issue during the Koizumi administration, writing,

> the idea that somehow the time consuming, messy business of making compromises in democratic political systems needs to be dispensed in favor of a more efficient, coherent policy making process. . . . [t]aken to its extreme . . . makes for an institutional arrangement that can undermine democracy itself.

Institutional Change, p. 8. He has made very similar observations about the Abe administration arguing,

> The concentration of power in the prime minister's office however brings with it its own dangers. . . . [N]ow that the prime minister's power over the cabinet and the party is so strong, the question arises where are the checks and balances necessary in a democratic polity going to come from? This question has taken on added urgency since it is not only the opposition parties that have become less vigorous but the liberal media as well.

Japan Update Speech, p. 7. See also Stockwin, Arthur and Ampiah, Kweku, *Rethinking Japan: The Politics of Contested Nationalism*, New York and London, Lexington Books, 2017.

Bibliography

'Abe Aims at Strong PM Office, Plans Tech-led Growth Strategy', *The Nikkei Weekly*, 2 October 2006, pp. 1, 3.

'"Abe ikkyō" no bōsō ni burēki o. Ryōshiki aru kokkai giin no hataraki sasaeru seron zukuri e, jūyō na JA gurūpu no kesshūryoku' ['Stop the Recklessness of "Abe as the Single Strong Figure". The JA Group's Uniting Power Is Important to Create Public Opinion that Supports the Work of Diet Members Who Have a Conscience'], *Nōsei Undō Jānaru*, No. 119, February 2015, p. 16.

'Abe Models Office on White House', *The Nikkei Weekly*, 2 October 2006, p. 2.

'Abe no saidai no seiteki wa "Suga Yoshihide", "Shukun to chūshin", Chikara kankei ga gyakuten suru hi' ['Abe's Biggest Political Rival Is "Yoshihide Suga", "Master and Loyal Retainer", The Day the Power Relationship Becomes Reversed'], *Sentaku*, November 2015, pp. 48–50.

'Abe's Decision to Tap Nikai for Important LDP Post Alarms Intraparty Rival Factions', *The Mainichi*, 2 August 2016, http://mainichi.jp/english/articles/20160802/p2a/00m/0na/015000c.

'Abe Shinzō ga kage no saishō Suga Yoshihide no "hanran" ni obie hajimeta, "Mō iiyo. Ore wa tsukareta"' ['Shinzō Abe Has Started to Become Scared of the "Rebellion" of Yoshihide Suga, the Prime Minister Behind the Curtain, "I Give Up. I'm Tired"'], *Shūkan Bijinesu*, 30 April edition, pp. 36–40, via *Gendai Bijinesu*, 25 April 2016, http://gendai.ismedia.jp/articles/-/48499.

Abe Shinzō o kangaeru kai, *Abe Shinzō to wa nanimono ka?* [*Who Is Shinzō Abe?*], Tokyo, Makino Shuppan, 2015.

Abe shushō no keizai seisaku burēn, Suisu taishi ni irei no tenshutsu Honda Etsurō naikaku kanbō sanyo' ['Prime Minister Abe's Economic Policy Brains and Special Advisor to the Cabinet Etsurō Honda Appointed as Ambassador to Switzerland in Exceptional Personnel Decision'], *Sankei Shinbun*, 11 March 2016, www.sankei.com/politics/news/160311/plt1603110032-n1.html.

'Abe's Power Play/Prime Minister Adept at Handling Personnel Matters of Factions', *Yomiuri Shimbun*, 8 March 2015, http://the-japan-news.com/news/article/0001985893.

'Abe's Unorthodox Policies Rooted in Distrust of Finance Ministry, BOJ', *Nikkei Asian Review*, 16 October 2016.

Aihara, Ryō, Myōraku, Asako, Oyamada, Kenji and Sumikawa, Takuya (eds), 'Nōkyō kaikaku, kōbō ga honkakuka, Jimin, Abenomikusu no shikinseki' ['Battle over JA Reform Shifts into Full Swing, the LDP's Touchstone for Abenomics'], *Asahi Shinbun Digital*, 21 January 2015, http://digital.asahi.com/articles/ASH1N3V8VH1NUTFK00H.html.

Aihara, Ryō and Oyamada, Kenji, '(Jiji kokukoku) Nōkyō kaikaku, seiken oshikiru, Zenchū no kengen, ōhaba shukushō' ['(Moment to Moment) Administration Overcomes Opposition to JA Reform, JA's Authority Significantly Reduced'], *Asahi Shinbun Digital*, 10 February 2015, http://digital.asahi.com/articles/DA3S11593742.html. 'Amari shi, tō sōmu ni shūnin, Yatō wa nao sekinin tsuikyū' ['Amari to Serve on LDP Executive Council, Opposition Parties Continue to Pursue His Responsibility'], *Nihon Keizai Shinbun*, 30 August 2016, p. 3.

Andō, Takeshi, 'Nōkyō kaikaku, "kyūtenkai" no wake, Kizukeba "shimensoka" no JA chūō soshiki' ['The Reason for the "Rapid Developments" in the Reforms to the JA, The JA's Central Organisations Found Themselves "Forsaken by Everyone"'], *Nikkei Business Online*, 20 May 2014, http://business.nikkeibp.co.jp/article/opinion/20140519/264917/.

Angel, Robert C., 'Prime Ministerial Leadership in Japan: Recent Changes in Personal Style and Administrative Organization', *Pacific Affairs*, Vol. 61, No. 4, Winter 1988–1989, pp. 583–602.

'Ano iwakutsuki no giin ga jūyō posuto de fukkatsu!' ['That Diet Member with a Past Was Revived in an Important Post!'], *President Online*, 15 June 2015, http://president.jp/articles/-/15367.

'Anpo "gōin ni oshikiri", Gekkanshi intabyū de Koizumi moto shushō' ['Security Legislation Was "Railroaded", Former Prime Minister Koizumi Says in Interview with Monthly Magazine'], *Asahi Shinbun Digital*, 10 December 2015, http://digital.asahi.com/articles/DA3S12109990.html.

Asano, Takaaki, 'Abenomikusu o sasaeru mittsu no seisaku kaigi' ['The Three Policy Councils That Support Abenomics'], *The Tokyo Foundation*, 2 July 2013 (Reproduced from *Bijinesu Hōmu*, July 2013 edition), www.tkfd.or.jp/research/project/news.php?id=1158.

'"Asō shi wa 'Abe sōri mo kodoku nanda' to" Kawamura giun iinchō' ['Lower House Steering Committee Chairman Kawamura Says, "Asō Said That 'Prime Minister Abe Is Isolated'"'], *Asahi Shinbun Digital*, 4 June 2016, www.asahi.com/articles/ASJ646589J64UTFK00D.html.

Cabinet Office, Outline of Duties, 2014, June 2014, www.cao.go.jp/en/pmf/about_pmf_index.pdf.

'Chūō shōchō jinji kantei shudō ga teichaku, Josei kanbu zōka "2 kaikyū tokushin" "Ishuku" kenen mo' ['Kantei Leadership over Personnel Affairs in Central Government Ministries and Agencies Established, Increase in Female Executives and "Promotion by Two Ranks", Concern over "Intimidation"'], *Yomiuri Shinbun*, 15 June 2016, p. 4.

Connors, Lesley, 'Next Steps for Japan: Administrative Reform and the Changing Policy', *Asia-Pacific Review*, Vol. 7, No. 1, 2000, pp. 109–130.

'Core Executive (UK Politics)', *tutor 2u*, www.tutor2u.net/politics/reference/core-executive-uk-politics.

Curtis, Gerald L., *Institutional Change and Political Reform: Back to Basics*, Discussion Paper No. 33, Discussion Paper Series, APEC Study Center, Columbia Business School, September 2004.

Curtis, Gerald L., *Japan Update Speech*, Paper delivered to the Japan Update Conference, Crawford School, Australian National University, Canberra, 21st September 2016.

'Dai 189 kai kokkai naikaku iinkai dai 23 gō' ['189th Diet Session Cabinet Committee No.23'], *Diet website*, 3 September 2015, http://kokkai.ndl.go.jp/SENTAKU/sangiin/189/0058/18909030058023a.html.

'Dai 3 ji saikaizō naikaku Saninsen "shinshō hitsubatsu" iro koku' ['Second Reshuffled Third Abe Cabinet Strongly Reflects Punishments and Rewards for Upper House Election'], *Sankei Shinbun* (Osaka HQ edition), 4 August 2016, pp. 1, 3, www.sankei.com/politics/news/160804/plt1608040007-n1.html.

The Democratic Party of Japan, *2009 Change of Government, The Democratic Party of Japan's Platform for Government*, www.dpj.or.jp/english/manifesto/manifesto2009.pdf.

Dowding, Keith, 'The Prime Ministerialisation of the British Prime Minister', *Parliamentary Affairs*, Vol. 13, 2013, pp. 617–635.

Dunleavy, Patrick and Rhodes, R.A.W., 'Core Executive Studies in Britain', *Public Administration*, Vol. 68, No. 1, March 1990, pp. 3–28.Estevez-Abe, Margarita, 'Japan's Shift Toward a Westminster System', *Asian Survey*, Vol. 46, No. 4, pp. 632–651.

Estevez-Abe, Margarita, Hikotani, Takako and Nagahisa, Toshio, 'Japan's New Executive Leadership: How Electoral Rules Make Japanese Security Policy', in Masaru Kohno and Frances Rosenbluth (eds), *Japan and the World: Japan's Contemporary Geopolitical Challenges*, New Haven, CT, Yale CEAS Occasional Publications, Volume 2, 2008, pp. 251–288.

Explaining Postal Reform in Japan, Monday, 11 June 2012, Center for East Asian Studies, University of Texas at Austin, https://liberalarts.utexas.edu/eastasia/news/article.php?id=5495.

Fackler, Martin, 'In Japan, a Leadership Vacuum', *New York Times*, 2 September 2008, www.nytimes.com/2008/09/03/world/asia/03japan.html.

Fukai, Shigeko N., 'The Missing Leader: The Structure and Traits of Political Leadership in Japan', in Feldman Ofer (ed.), *Political Psychology in Japan*, Nova Science Publishers, Inc., Commack, New York, 1998, pp. 171–191.

Furukawa, Teijirō, 'Sōri kantei to kanbō no kenkyū – Taiken ni motozuite' ['A Study of the Prime Minister's Official Residence and Secretariat – Based on Experience'], *Nenpo Gyōsei Kenkyū*, Vol. 2005, No. 40, 2005, www.jstage.jst.go.jp/article/jspa1962/2005/40/2005_2/_pdf.

Gannon, James and Sahashi, Ryo, 'Looking for Leadership', in Ryo Sahashi and James Gannon (eds), *Looking for Leadership: The Dilemma of Political Leadership in Japan*, Tokyo and New York, Japan Center for International Exchange, 2015, pp. 11–28.

Gaunder, Alisa, *Political Reform in Japan: Leadership Looming Large*, Abingdon and New York, Routledge, 2007.

George Mulgan, Aurelia, *An Overview of Japanese Politics*, Paper presented to the Japanese Economic and Management Studies Centre, University of New South Wales 'Understanding Japan Today' series, 3 November 1992.

George Mulgan, Aurelia, 'Japan's Political Leadership Deficit', *Australian Journal of Political Science*, Vol. 3, No. 2, 2000, pp. 183–202.

George Mulgan, Aurelia, *Japan's Failed Revolution: Koizumi and the Politics of Economic Reform*, Canberra, ANU Press, 2002.George Mulgan, Aurelia, 'Japan's "Un-Westminster" System: Impediments to Reform in a Crisis Economy', *Government and Opposition*, Vol. 38, No. 1, January 2003, pp. 73–91.

George Mulgan, Aurelia, 'Where Tradition Meets Change: Japan's Agricultural Politics in Transition', *Journal of Japanese Studies*, Vol. 31, No. 2, Summer 2005, pp. 261–298.

George Mulgan, Aurelia, 'The Politics of Economic Reform', in Alisa Gaunder (ed.), *The Routledge Handbook of Japanese Politics*, London and New York, Routledge, 2011, pp. 261–272.

George Mulgan, Aurelia, "Agriculture", in James Babb (ed.), *Handbook of Modern Japanese Studies*, Sage, Thousand Oaks, CA, 2015, pp. 737–761.

George Mulgan, Aurelia, 'Loosening the Ties That Bind: Japan's Agricultural Policy Triangle and Reform of Cooperatives (JA)', *Journal of Japanese Studies*, Vol. 42, No. 2, Summer 2016, pp. 221–246.

George Mulgan, Aurelia, 'Securitizing the TPP in Japan: Policymaking Structure and Discourse', *Asia Policy*, 22, July 2016, pp. 193–221.

George Mulgan, Aurelia, 'Media Muzzling under the Abe Administration', in Jeff Kingston (ed.), *Press Freedom in Contemporary Japan*, London and New York, Routledge, 2017, pp. 17–29.

Grube, Dennis C. and Howard, Cosmo, 'Is the Westminster System Broken beyond Repair?', *Governance*, Vol. 29, No. 4, October 2016, pp. 467–481.

Hanatani, Mie, '"Kantei ikkyō" no iroai tsuyomaru keizai seisaku no kettei' ['Kantei Dominates Economic Policymaking under the Abe Administration'], *Ekonomisuto*, 10 May 2016, p. 25.

'Hatsu taidan dokusen 70 pun, Suga *kanbō chōkan* Toranpu daitōryō no tsuittā, keizai seisaku wa tegowai, Nikai kajichō Koike san wa wareware to hantai no koto o suru to omotte chōdo ii, Toranpu daitōryō, Koike gekijō, postuo Abe, tennō taii, kaisan senryaku, "amakudari" o katatta' ['First 70-Minute Exclusive Joint Interview, Chief Cabinet Secretary Suga: "President Trump's Twitter and Economic Policies Are Tough Issues", Secretary-General Nikai: "You Can Assume That Koike Will Do the Opposite of What We Do", Discussions on President Trump, the Koike Theatre, Post-Abe, Emperor's Abdication, Dissolution Strategy, and "Amakudari"'], *Shūkan Asahi*, 17 February 2017, pp. 24–27.

Hayao, Kenji, *The Japanese Prime Minister and Public Policy*, Pittsburgh, PA, University of Pittsburgh Press, 1993.

Heffernan, Richard, *Presidentialization in the United Kingdom: Prime Ministerial Power and Parliamentary Democracy*, Paper prepared for delivery at the 28th Joint Sessions of Workshops of the European Consortium of Political Research, University of Copenhagen, 14 to 19 April 2000, https://ecpr.eu/Filestore/PaperProposal/9c85aa57-e9c7-45b9-bd92-2eb41282e737.pdf.

Hosoya, Yuichi, 'The Evolution of Japan's "Leadership Deficit"', in Ryo Sahashi and James Gannon (eds), *Looking for Leadership: The Dilemma of Political Leadership in Japan*, Tokyo and New York, Japan Center for International Exchange, 2015, pp. 31–45.

Iida, Yasumichi, *JA Kaitai – 1000 man kumiaiin no meiun* [*Dissolution of JA – The Fate of the 10 Million Members*], Tokyo, Tōyō Keizai Shinpōsha, 2015.

Iinuma, Yoshisuke, 'Abe's New Conservatism: Flood of New Diet Members Decimates LDP "Old Guard"', *The Oriental Economist Report*, Vol. 84, No. 3, March 2016, pp. 11–13.

Iio, Jun, *Nihon no tōchi kōzō: Kanryō naikakusei kara giin naikakusei e* [*Japan's Structure of Governance: From a Bureaucratic to a Parliamentary Cabinet System*], Tokyo, Chūō Kōron Shinsha, 2007.

Iizuka, Keiko and Smith, Sheila A., 'Who Is Shinzo Abe?', *Council on Foreign Relations*, CFT Events, 15 May 2015, www.cfr.org/japan/shinzo-abe/p36523.

'"Itsuka seiken o" Kishida shi ga iyoku' ['Kishida Indicates Desire to "One Day Take the Reins of Government"'], *Tokyo Shimbun*, 7 September 2016, p. 6.

'Jimin, seisaku kettei ni "ihen", Yosan, zeisei de tetsuzuki kanryakuka aitsugu' ['"Anomaly" in LDP's Policymaking, Procedure Simplified in Relation to Budget and Taxation'], *Nihon Keizai Shinbun* (electronic edition), 30 August 2013, www.nikkei.com/article/DGXNASFS29029_Z20C13A8PP8000/.

'Jimintō – Shuyō yakuin, habatsu baransu jūshi, "Kantei shudō" iji ni fushin' ['LDP – Factional Balance Emphasised in Appointment of Main Party Executives, Efforts Made to Maintain "Kantei Leadership"'], *Mainichi Shinbun*, 4 August 2016, p. 5.

Kaihara, Hiroshi, 'The Advent of a New Japanese Politics: Effects of the 1994 Revision of the Electoral Law', *Asian Survey*, Vol. 47, No. 5, 2007, pp. 749–765.

'Kantei no sekkyoku zaisei rosen ni kasei Nikai shi, hatafuriyaku ni' ['Nikai Appointed as a Flag-bearer to Support Kantei's Expansionary Fiscal Policy Line'] *Nihon Keizai Shinbun*, 1 September 2016, p. 3.

'Kantei shudō ga irokoku, 16 nendo yosanan, Saninsen e gyōkai hairyo' ['Strong Characteristics of Kantei's Leadership, Budget Proposal for Fiscal 2016 Shows Consideration for Industries in Preparation for Upper House Election'], *Nihon Keizai Shinbun*, 25 December 2015, www.nikkei.com/article/DGXLZO95520470V21C15A2EA1000/.

'Kantei shudō seiji ni, tō, kokkai ga sonzaikan o hakki' ['The Party and the Diet Exert a Strong Presence in Kantei-led Politics'], *Nōsei Undō Jānaru*, No. 112, December 2013, p. 17.

'[Kataru] 15 nen seiji tenbō Anpo hōsei Ji Kō no sa wa umaru Kōmura Masahiko shi' ['[Talk] Political Landscape in 2015, The Gap over Security Legislation between LDP and Kōmeitō Can Be Closed, Kōmura Masahiko'], *Yomiuri Shinbun*, 13 February 2015, p. 4.

Katō, Hideki, 'Political Reform of the Japanese System of Government (Symposium Report 2)', *Tokyo Foundation*, 28 October 2008, www.tokyofoundation.org/en/articles/2008/political-reform-of-the-japanese-system-of-government-symposium-report-2.

Katz, Rick, 'So Strong and Yet So Weak: Abe's Approval: A Mile Wide, Just an Inch Deep', *The Oriental Economist Report*, Vol. 84, No. 3, March 2016, pp. 1–2.

'Kenshō manatsu no jinji (jō) "Ikkyō" shushō no gosan' ['Analysis of the Mid-summer Personnel Affairs (Part 1) The Miscalculation of the "Single Strong" Prime Minister'], *Nihon Keizai Shinbun*, 5 August 2016, p. 4.

'Kigyō no nōchi shoyū nin'yō, Gōin na kanwa wa kōka ni gimon, Nōka fushinkan, dashishiburi ni hakusha mo' ['Effects of Forcibly Relaxing Regulations to Allow Farmland Ownership by Companies Questionable, It May Breed Distrust among Farmers and Encourage Them to Hold Onto Their Land'], *Sankei Shinbun*, 3 March 2016, p. 11.

Kingston, Jeff, 'Abe's Faltering Efforts to Restart Japan', *Current History*, September 2016, pp. 233–239.

'[Kinkyū intabyū Keizai hyōronka Uchihashi Katsuto shi ni kiku (jō)] "Nōkyō kai-kaku" o kiru, hihan seishin tsuyome taikōjiku o' ['[Emergency Interview with Economic Critic Uchihashi Katsuto (Part 1)] Criticising the "Agricultural Cooperative Reform"; Strengthen Critical Mindset and Build Foundation for Opposition'], *JAcom*, 30 November 2016, www.jacom.or.jp/nousei/closeup/2016/161130-31506.php.

Kishi, Hiroyuki, 'Nōgyō kaikaku wa doko made jitsugen suru ka' ['To What Extent Will the Agricultural Reforms Be Realised?'], *Diamond Online*, No. 265, 23 May 2014, http://diamond.jp/articles/-/53453.

'Koizumi Shinjirō shi, mata nanyaku, Nōgyō ni tsuzuki shakai hoshō kirikomi, Kōrō zoku "giron suru dake"' ['Shinjirō Koizumi Given Another Tough Job to Delve into Social Security Following Agriculture, Health, Labour and Welfare Tribe Diet Members Say "It Will Be All Talk"'], *Sankei Shinbun*, 4 February 2016, p. 5.

'Kokka kōmuin no teiin (Heisei 13 nendo-28 nendo)' ['Number of National Public Servants (FY 2001-FY 2016)'], *Cabinet Secretariat website*, www.cas.go.jp/jp/gaiyou/jimu/jinjikyoku/files/h280401_teiin.xlsx.

'Kokunai jinji jōhō' ['Information on Domestic Personnel Affairs'], *Sentaku*, May 2016, p. 11.

Krauss, Ellis S. and Nyblade, Benjamin, '"Presidentialization" in Japan? The Prime Minister, Media and Elections in Japan', *British Journal of Political Science*, Vol. 35, No. 2, April 2005, pp. 357–368.

Krauss, Ellis S. and Pekkanen, Robert J., *The Rise and Fall of Japan's LDP: Political Party Organizations as Historical Institutions*, Ithaca, NY, Cornell University Press, 2010.

Liberal Democratic Party of Japan, 'Chapter Eleven, Period of President Nakasone's Leadership', *A History of the Liberal Democratic Party*, www.jimin.jp/english/about-ldp/history/104291.html.

Liberal Democratic Party of Japan, *Official English Translations for LDP Officials and Party Organs*, www.jimin.jp/english/profile/english/.

Machidori, Satoshi, *Shushō seiji no seido bunseki: Gendai Nihon seiji no kenryoku kiban keisei* [*The Japanese Premiership: An Institutional Analysis of the Power Relations*], Tokyo, Chikura Shobō, 2012.

Maclachlan, Patricia, *The People's Post Office: The History and Politics of the Japanese Postal System, 1871–2010*, Cambridge, MA, Harvard University Press, 2012.

Maki, John M., 'Executive Power in Japan', *Far Eastern Survey*, Vol. 24, No. 5, May 1955, pp. 71–75.

Makihara, Izuru, 'Seisaku kettei ni okeru shushō kantei no yakuwari' ['The Role of the Kantei in Making Policy'], *Nippon.com*, 27 June 2013, www.nippon.com/ja/features/c00408/.

Makihara, Izuru, 'The Role of the Kantei in Making Policy', *Nippon.com*, 7 August 2013, www.nippon.com/en/features/c00408/.

Makihara, Izuru, 'Abe's Enforcer: Suga Yoshihide's Stabilizing Influence on the Cabinet', *Nippon.com*, 25 September 2014, www.nippon.com/en/currents/d00135/.

Masuyama, Mikitaka and Nyblade, Benjamin, 'Japan: The Prime Minister and the Japanese Diet', *The Journal of Legislative Studies*, Vol. 10, No. 2/3, Summer/Autumn 2004, pp. 250–262.

McEwen, Nicola, 'Power within the Executive', Unit 2, Governing the UK, *BBC News*, 1 September 2003, http://news.bbc.co.uk/2/hi/programmes/bbc_parliament/2561931.stm.

'Menkai ōi aite wa? Abe shushō no 4 nenkan, dēta de kaibō' ['Who Meets Abe Most? An Analysis of Data on Abe's Four Years as Prime Minister'], *Nihon Keizai Shinbun*, 29 January 2017, www.nikkei.com/article/DGXLZO12255640Y7A120C1TZJ000/.

Mikuriya, Takashi, *Abe seiken wa hontō ni tsuyoi no ka* [*Is the Abe Administration Actually Strong?*], Tokyo, PHP Kenkyūjo, 2015.

Minami, Akira, 'Kasumigaseki no meishu, Zaimushō kara Keisanshō e Shushō sokkin ni shusshinsha' ['The Ministry of Economy, Trade and Industry Wrests Kasumigaseki Crown from the Ministry of Finance, Supplying Bureaucrats for Positions Close to Abe'], *Asahi Shinbun Digital*, 28 February 2017, www.asahi.com/articles/ASK2S43XWK2SUTFK012.html.

Mishima, Ko, 'Grading Japanese Prime Minister Koizumi's Revolution', *Asian Survey*, Vol. 47, No. 5, 2007, pp. 727–748.

Miura, Ruri, 'Nōkyō kaikaku no tsugi ni kuru mono' ['What Will Come after the JA Reform'], *Miura Ruri blog*, 11 February 2015, http://lullymiura.hatenadiary.jp/entry/2015/02/11/212157.

Mochizuki, Mike M., 'Japan's Long Transition: The Politics of Recalibrating Grand Strategy', in Ashley J. Tellis and Michael Wills (eds), *Domestic Political Change and Grand Strategy, Strategic Asia 2007–08*, Seattle, The National Bureau of Asian Research, 2007, pp. 67–111.

Mori, Satoru, 'Political Leadership in Japan and Japanese Foreign Policy: Lessons from the DPJ Governments', in Ryo Sahashi and James Gannon (eds), *Looking for Leadership: The Dilemma of Political Leadership in Japan*, Tokyo and New York, Japan Center for International Exchange, 2015, pp. 159–177.

'Movers of Abe's Diplomacy', *Sentaku*, 11 February 2013, www.japantimes.co.jp/opinion/2013/02/11/commentary/japan-commentary/movers-of-abes-diplomacy/.

Mughan, Anthony, *Media and the Presidentialization of Parliamentary Election*, New York, Palgrave, 2000.

Naikakuhō [*Cabinet Law*], http://law.e-gov.go.jp/htmldata/S22/S22HO005.html.

'Naikaku kaizō e omowaku kōsaku, Suga, Asō shi ryūnin e, Kokkaku iji' ['Intentions Intertwine Ahead of Cabinet Reshuffle, Suga and Asō to Keep Posts, Administration's Framework to Be Maintained'], *Nihon Keizai Shinbun*, 26 July 2016, www.nikkei.com/article/DGXLASDE25H09_V20C16A7PP8000/.

'Naikaku kanbō no kenkyū (chū) Kakushō kara ēsu kanryō, Kantei no ikō, jinsoku ni jitsugen' ['A Study of the Cabinet Secretariat (Part 2): Bringing in Ace Bureaucrats from Various Ministries to Swiftly Realise What the Kantei Wants'], *Nihon Keizai Shinbun*, 19 April 2017, p. 4.

'Naikaku kanbō no kenkyū (ge): Shōchō jinji mo kantei shudō', Kado na sontaku umu kenen' ['A Study of the Cabinet Secretariat (Part 3): Kantei Controls Appointments in the Ministries, Concern That It May Lead to Excessively Surmising the Kantei's Intentions'], *Nihon Keizai Shinbun*, 21 April 2017, p. 4.

'Naikaku kanbō no kenkyū (jō), Kantei shūken shōchō wa teashi, Hatarakikata kaikaku, tai Bei kōshō . . . Omo na seisaku dokusen, "chōsei dake" ima wa mukashi' ['A Study of the Cabinet Secretariat (Part 1): Concentration of Power in the Kantei with the Ministries at their Beck and Call, Work Style Reform, Negotiations with the US . . . Kantei Monopolises Major Policies, "Only Working on Coordination" Is Something of the Past'], *Nihon Keizai Shinbun*, 18 April 2017, p. 4.

Nakasone, Yasuhiro, 'Pitchers and Catchers: Politicians, Bureaucrats, and Policy-Making in Japan', *Asia-Pacific Review*, Vol. 2, No. 1, 1995, p. 5–14.

National Science Foundation, Tokyo Regional Office, Report Memorandum #01–02, *Central Government Reform in Japan: Rationale and Prospects*, 9 February 2001, www.nsf.gov/od/oise/tokyo/reports/trm/rm01-02.html.

NHK News 7, 6 March 2017.

NHK News 7, 27 October 2016.

Nihon keizai zaisei honbu meibo [*Headquarters for Japan's Economic Revitalisation Membership List*], 1 September 2016, www.kantei.go.jp/jp/singi/keizaisaisei/pdf/meibo.pdf.

'Nishikawa moto Nōsuishō TPP "uchimaku bon" no zenbun nyūshu, "Abe shushō 'Zoku o motte zoku o seisu'"' ['Full Text of Former MAFF Minister Nishikawa's "Book on the Inside Story" of the TPP Obtained, "Prime Minister Abe Said 'Fight Tribe Diet Members with Tribe Diet Members'"'], *dot.*, 20 April 2016, http://dot.asahi.com/wa/2016041900209.html.

Noble, Gregory W., 'Seijiteki rīdāshippu to kōzō kaikaku' ['Political Leadership and Structural Reform'], in Tōkyō Daigaku Shakai Kagaku Kenkyūjo (ed.), *Ushinawareta 10 nen o koete (II) Koizumi kaikaku no jidai e* [*Beyond the Lost Decade (II) Toward the Age of Koizumi Reform*], Tokyo, Tōkyō Daigaku Shuppankai, 2006.

Nogami, Tadaoki, '"Shunki kiki" setsu, fujō – Saga shokku no seiken ni' ['"Spring Crisis" Theory Surfaces – As Administration Deals with the Saga Shock'], *Nōsei Undō Jānaru*, No. 119, February 2015, pp. 8–9.

'Nōkyō kaikaku, ganban kuzushi e kantei no shūnen, Saga chijisen no haiboku no bane' ['JA Reform, The Kantei's Tenacity in Undermining the Bedrock, The Kantei Sprung Back from Defeat in the Saga Gubernatorial Election'], *Nihon Keizai Shinbun*, 10 February 2015, www.nikkei.com/article/DGXLASFS09H7E_Z00C15A2EA2000/.

'Nōsei kaikaku, naru ka Shinjirō ryū, Teikō seiryoku ni kirikomu (Shinsō shinsō)' ['Will Shinjirō's Agricultural Policy Reform Produce Results? Cutting into the Resistance Force (Depths of Truth)'], *Nihon Keizai Shinbun*, 3 February 2016, p. 2.

'Nōsui fukudaijin, seimukan, keisanzoku zurari, Kaikaku jinarashi? Hirogaru hamon' ['METI Tribe Diet Members Fill MAFF State Minister and Parliamentary Vice-Minister Posts, Is It Groundwork for Reform? Appointment Causes Stir'], *Nihon Keizai Shinbun*, 6 August 2016, p. 4.

Nyblade, Benjamin, 'The 21st Century Japanese Prime Minister: An Unusually Precarious Perch', *Journal of Social Science*, Vol. 61, No. 2, February 2011, pp. 195–209.

Ogawa, Mayumi, 'Koizumi Shinjirō Jimin nōrin bukaichō "hitoyose panda" o sotsugyō? Nōgyō kaikaku de shuwan apīru, Shūi kara "dekirēsu" no kageguchi mo . . .' ['Has LDP Agriculture and Forestry Division Director Koizumi Shinjirō Become More Than a "Crowd Puller"? Koizumi Emphasises His Skills in Relation to Agricultural Reform, Some People Talk Behind His Back That It Was a "Fixed Game" . . .'], *Sankei News*, 2 December 2016, www.sankei.com/premium/news/161202/prm1612020007-n1.html.

'Omo na honbu-kaigitai' ['Main Headquarters and Council Bodies'], *Shushō kantei* [*Prime Minister of Japan and His Cabinet*], www.kantei.go.jp/jp/singi/index.html.

'Oshikomareta Jimin zeichō, Shushōgawa kōsei, taichō ichidan to' ['LDP Tax Research Commission Pushed Back, Prime Minister's Side Takes the Offensive, LDP Retreats Further'], *Nihon Keizai Shinbun*, 31 December 2014, www.nikkei.com/article/DGXLASFS30H5L_Q4A231C1EA1000/

Ōtake, Hideo, *Koizumi Junichirō popyurizumu no kenkyū* [*A Study of Koizumi Junichirō's Populism*], Tokyo, Tōyō Keizai Shinpōsha, 2006.

'Overview: The Cabinet Office's Role in the Cabinet', *Cabinet Office, Outline of Duties 2014*, www.cao.go.jp/en/pmf/pmf_about.pdf.

Ozawa, Ichirō, *Blueprint for a New Japan: The Rethinking of a Nation*, Tokyo, Kōdansha International, 1994.

Pempel, T. J., 'Between Pork and Productivity: The Collapse of the Liberal Democratic Party', *Journal of Japanese Studies*, Vol. 36, No. 2, Summer 2010, pp. 227–254.

Prime Minister of Japan and His Cabinet, *Press Conference by the Chief Cabinet Secretary*, Tuesday, 7 January 2014 (AM), http://japan.kantei.go.jp/tyoukanpress/201401/07_a.html.

Richardson, Bradley, *Japanese Democracy: Power, Coordination, and Performance*, New Haven, CT, Yale University Press, 1997.

Sakano, Tomokazu, *The Presidentialization of Politics in Britain and Japan: Comparing Party Responses to Electoral Dealignment*, Paper presented at the 2006 IPSA World Congress, Fukuoka, Japan, 10–14 July 2006.

'Seiji jōhō kapuseru' ['Politics: Information Capsule'], *Sentaku*, July 2016, p. 45.

'[Seiji no genba] Chōki seiken no tenbō (4) Jinji nigiri kanryō o "saiten"' ['[The Grassroots of Politics] The Long-term Administration's Vision (4) "Grade" Bureaucrats by Controlling Personnel Decisions'], *Yomiuri Shinbun*, 2 December 2016, p. 4.

Shimizu, Masato, *Kantei shudō: Koizumi Junichirō no kakumei* [*Kantei Leadership: The Revolution of Koizumi Jun'ichirō*], Tokyo, Nihon Keizai Shinbunsha, 2005.

Shimizu, Masato, *Keizai zaisei senki – Kantei shudō Koizumi kara Abe e* [*History of the Economic and Fiscal War – Kantei Leadership, from Koizumi to Abe*], Tokyo, Nihon Keizai Shinbun Shuppansha, 2007.

Shinoda, Tomohito, 'Japan's Cabinet Secretariat and Its Emergence as Core Executive', *Asian Survey*, Vol. 45, No. 5, 2005, pp. 800–821.

Shinoda, Tomohito, 'Japan's Top-Down Policy Process to Dispatch the SDF to Iraq', *Japanese Journal of Political Science*, Vol. 7, No. 1, 2006, pp. 71–91.

Shinoda, Tomohito, *Koizumi Diplomacy: Japan's Kantei Approach to Foreign and Defense Affairs*, Seattle and London, University of Washington Press, 2007.

Shinoda, Tomohito, 'Koizumi's Top-Down Leadership in the Anti-Terrorism Legislation: the Impact of Political Institutional Changes', *SAIS Review 23*, No. 1, Winter/Spring 2003, pp. 19–34.

Shinoda, Tomohito, *Leading Japan: The Role of the Prime Minister*, Westport, Praeger, 2000.

Shinoda, Tomohito, 'Prime Ministerial Leadership', in Alisa Gaunder (ed.), *The Routledge Handbook of Japanese Politics*, London and New York, Routledge, 2011, pp. 48–59.

Shinoda, Tomohito, 'Stronger Political Leadership and the Shift in Policy-making Boundaries in Japan', in Glenn D. Hook (ed.), *Decoding Boundaries in Contemporary Japan: The Koizumi Administration and Beyond*, London and New York, Routledge, 2011, pp. 101–119.

Shiozaki, Yasuhisa, 'Changes in the Japanese Policymaking Process', in Thomas E. Mann and Takeshi Sasaki (eds), *Governance for a New Century: Japanese Challenges, American Experience*, Tokyo, Japan Center for International Exchange, 2002, pp. 53–62.

'Shushō, jizen no jūryōkyū kiyō, Jimin kanjichō ni Nikai shi, "Sōsai ninki enchō e no fuseki" to no mikata ['Prime Minister Settles for Second Best Heavyweight Nikai as LDP Secretary-General, Views That It Is a "Preparatory Step for Extending His Term of Office as LDP Leader"'], *Nihon Keizai Shinbun*, 2 August 2016, p. 4.

'Shushō kantei no media kōryaku jutsu' ['The Kantei's Media Strategy'], *Shūkan Tōyō Keizai*, 12 December 2015, pp. 48–51.

'Shushō no "otomodachi" Yamamoto Yūji Nōsuishō, Ishiba ha de wa uragirimono no yuda' ['Prime Minister's "Friend", MAFF Minister Yūji Yamamoto, Yamamoto Is the Ishiba Faction's Judas'], *Nikkan Gendai*, 15 August 2016, www.nikkan-gendai.com/articles/view/news/187792.

'Shushō no shinanyaku Hamada kyōju ga GPIF kabu tōshi "ōzon" no gyōten hatsugen' ['Prime Minister's Mentor, Professor Hamada Makes Shocking Comment on GPIF Stock Investments Resulting in Potential "Major Losses"'], *Nikkan Gendai*, 19 January 2016, www.nikkan-gendai.com/articles/view/news/173564.

'Shushō sasaeru "kuroko" goninshū hosakan, jitsumu jūshi no jogenyaku, gaikō, kōhō . . . senmon bunya ikasu' ['The Five "Unsung Heroes" Who Support Abe, Advisors' Emphasis on Practical Work, Effectively Use Specialised Skills in Diplomacy, PR etc.'], *Nihon Keizai Shinbun*, 17 June 2016, p. 2, www.nikkei.com/article/DGKKZO03723970X10C16A6EAC000/.

'Shushō tōben, tsuyoki no wake, Yatō tsuikyū mae ni sente' ['The Reason Behind Prime Minister Abe's Confidence in Responding to Questions in the Diet, He Forestalls the Opposition Parties Before They Start Questioning'], *Nihon Keizai Shinbun*, 28 January 2017, www.nikkei.com/article/DGXLASFS27H56_X20C17A1PP8000/.

Stockwin, Arthur and Ampiah, Kweku, *Rethinking Japan: The Politics of Contested Nationalism*, New York and London, Lexington Books, 2017.

Stockwin, J.A.A., *Dictionary of the Modern Politics of Japan*, London and New York, Routledge, 2003.

Stockwin, J.A.A., *Governing Japan: Divided Politics in a Major Economy*, 3rd edn. Oxford, Blackwell, 1999.

'Suga *kanbō chōkan* zaishoku saichō ni 1290 nichi, Fukuda Yasuo shi o nuku' ['Suga Becomes the Longest Serving Chief Cabinet Secretary at 1290 Days, Breaks Yasuo Fukuda's Record'], *Asahi Shinbun*, 7 July 2016, p. 4.

Sugiura, Nobuhiko, *JA ga kawareba Nihon no nōgyō wa tsuyoku naru* [*Japan's Agricultural Industry Will Become Stronger If JA Changes*], Tokyo, Discover21, 2015.

Suzuki, Tetsuo, '*Kaibō seikai kīman* Suga Yoshihide *kanbō chōkan* Kasumigaseki ni nirami o kikasu "jinji" to seiken sasaeru "shoku ni tessuru"' ['*Dissecting Key Political Figures* Chief Cabinet Secretary Yoshihide Suga: Use "Personnel Affairs" to Exert Pressure Against Kasumigaseki and "Devote All Efforts to the Job" to Support the Administration'], Zakzak by *Yūkan Fuji*, 13 August 2016, www.zakzak.co.jp/society/politics/news/20160813/plt1608131000002-n1.htm.

Takayasu, Kensuke, 'Prime-Ministerial Power in Japan: A Re-Examination', *Japan Forum*, Vol. 17, No. 2, 2005, pp. 163–184.

Takayasu, Kensuke, 'The Pressures of Change: The Office of Prime Minister in the United Kingdom and Japan', *Nippon.com*, 21 May 2014, www.nippon.com/en/features/c00410/.

Takenaka, Harukata, *Shushō shihai: Nihon seiji no henbō* [*Prime Ministerial Rule: The Transformation of Japanese Politics*], Tokyo, Chūō Kōron Shinsha, 2006.

Takenaka, Harukata, 'The Frequent Turnover of Japanese Prime Ministers: Still a Long Way to a Westminster Model', in Ryo Sahashi and James Gannon (eds), *Looking for Leadership: The Dilemma of Political Leadership in Japan*, Tokyo and New York, Japan Center for International Exchange, 2015, pp. 46–82.

Takenaka, Heizō, 'Abe seiken no seisaku kettei purosesu' ['The Abe Administration's Policymaking Process'], Japan Center for Economic Research (An Article for the Series "Takenaka Heizō no Porishī Sukūru" ["Heizō Takenaka's Policy School"]), 26 November 2013, www.jcer.or.jp/column/takenaka/index565.html.

'Tanigaki kokete haran, Abe shushō ga Ima kangaete Iru "gyōten jinji"' ['Tanigaki's Fall Causes a Commotion; The "Surprise Personnel Decisions" That Prime Minister Abe Is Thinking about Right Now'], *Shūkan Gendai*, 6 August 2016, p. 76.

'[Tantō chokugen] Hagiuda Kōichi kanbō fukuchōkan, "Abe ikkyō" nani ga waruin desu ka' ['[Point-Blank Comment] Deputy Chief Cabinet Secretary Kōichi Hagiuda Asks What Is Wrong with Abe Seizing "Unrivalled Control"'], *Sankei Shinbun*, 24 April 2017, p. 5.

Taoka, Shunji, 'Chūgoku gunkan no setsuzoku suiiki kōkō e no kōgi wa jibun no kubi o shimeru kōi' ['The Government Is Digging Their Own Grave by Protesting the Chinese Naval Vessels Entering the Contiguous Zone'], *Diamond Online*, 16 June 2016, http://diamond.jp/articles/-/93104.

Tazaki, Shirō, *Abe kantei no shōtai* [*The Truth about Abe's Kantei*], Tokyo, Kōdansha, 2014.

Tazaki, Shirō, 'JA Zenchū ga enjita Zaimushō no ni no mai, Abe kantei ni "sotobori senpō" wa tsūjizu' ['The Central Union of Agricultural Cooperatives Followed in the Footsteps of the Ministry of Finance, The "Tactic of Encircling the Kantei" Did Not Work'], *Gendai Business*, 9 February 2015, http://gendai.ismedia.jp/articles/-/42013.

Tokuyama, Jirō, 'Japan's Leaderless State', *Japan Echo*, Vol. 18, No. 4, 1991, pp. 35–41.

Toshikawa, Takao, 'MOF Loses Tax Fight to Abe: Kantei Asserts Its Power', *The Oriental Economist Report*, Vol. 84, No. 1, January 2016, pp. 4–5.

Toshikawa, Takao, 'Upper House Election Prospects: Why No "Double Election" This Year', *The Oriental Economist Report*, Vol. 84, No. 6, June 2016, p. 4.

Uchiyama, Yū, *Koizumi and Japanese Politics: Reform Strategies and Leadership Style*, Trans. Carl Freire, New York and London, Routledge, 2010.

Uchiyama, Yū, 'Nihon seiji no akutā to seisaku kettei patān' ['Actors and Policy-making Patterns in Japanese Politics'], *Kikan Seisaku Keiei Kenkyū*, Vol. 3, Mitsubishi UFJ Research and Consulting, 2010, www.murc.jp/english/think_tank/quarterly_journal/qj1003_01.pdf.

Van Wolferen, Karel, *The Enigma of Japanese Power*, New York, Vintage Books, 1990.

Woodall, Brian, *Growing Democracy in Japan: The Parliamentary Cabinet System Since 1868*, Lexington, University Press of Kentucky, 2014.

Yamashita, Kazuhito, 'TPP hantairon wa ronri hatan shite iru' ['The Anti-TPP Logic Is Full of Holes'], *Webronza*, 21 October 2016, http://webronza.asahi.com/business/articles/2016102000003.html

Yoshida, Reiji, 'Nishimuro Tapped to Take over Japan Post, Move Shows LDP Coalition's Bid for Influence', *The Japan Times*, 11 May 2013, www.japantimes.co.jp/news/2013/05/11/business/nishimuro-tapped-to-take-over-japan-post/#.WAnCXISRC-I.

'Zeichō innā ni Amari shi ga kanyū e' ['Amari to Join "Inner Circle" of LDP Tax Commission'], *Yomiuri Shinbun*, 24 September 2016, p. 4.

Index

For Product Safety Concerns and Information please contact our EU
representative GPSR@taylorandfrancis.com
Taylor & Francis Verlag GmbH, Kaufingerstraße 24, 80331 München, Germany

www.ingramcontent.com/pod-product-compliance
Ingram Content Group UK Ltd.
Pitfield, Milton Keynes, MK11 3LW, UK
UKHW021422080625
459435UK00011B/113